The Art of War

CUPPA CLASSICS

The Art of War

Sun Tzŭ

THE BROWSER

Title: The Art of War
Author: Sun Tzŭ

ISBN:978-93-92210-79-2
Imprint: The Browser | Cuppa Classics

Published by:
JGS Enterprises Pvt Ltd
SCO 14-15, FF, Sector 8-C,
Chandigarh 160 009
Website: cuppaclassics.com
Email: service@thebrowser.org

First Published in antiquity
This edition is published by The Browser in 2025
Printed in India

THE BROWSER

Contents

Preface

by Lionel Giles

The seventh volume of *Mémoires concernant l'histoire, les sciences, les arts, les moeurs, les usages, &c., des Chinois* is devoted to the Art of War, and contains, amongst other treatises, "Les Treize Articles de Sun-tse," translated from the Chinese by a Jesuit Father, Joseph Amiot. Père Amiot appears to have enjoyed no small reputation as a sinologue in his day, and the field of his labours was certainly extensive. But his so-called translation of the Sun Tzŭ, if placed side by side with the original, is seen at once to be little better than an imposture. It contains a great deal that Sun Tzŭ did not write, and very little indeed of what he did. Here is a fair specimen, taken from the opening sentences of chapter 5:—

> *De l'habileté dans le gouvernement des Troupes.* Sun-tse dit: Ayez les noms de tous les Officiers tant généraux que subalternes; inscrivez-les dans un catalogue à part, avec la note des talents & de la capacité de chacun d'eux, afin de pouvoir les employer avec avantage lorsque l'occasion en sera venue. Faites en sorte que tous ceux que vous devez commander soient persuadés que votre principale attention est de les préserver de tout dommage. Les troupes que vous ferez avancer contre l'ennemi doivent être comme des pierres que vous lanceriez contre des œufs. De vous à

> l'ennemi il ne doit y avoir d'autre différence que celle du fort au faible, du vide au plein. Attaquez à découvert, mais soyez vainqueur en secret. Voilà en peu de mots en quoi consiste l'habileté & toute la perfection même du gouvernement des troupes.

Throughout the nineteenth century, which saw a wonderful development in the study of Chinese literature, no translator ventured to tackle Sun Tzŭ, although his work was known to be highly valued in China as by far the oldest and best compendium of military science. It was not until the year 1905 that the first English translation, by Capt. E.F. Calthrop. R.F.A., appeared at Tokyo under the title "Sonshi"(the Japanese form of Sun Tzŭ). Unfortunately, it was evident that the translator's knowledge of Chinese was far too scanty to fit him to grapple with the manifold difficulties of Sun Tzŭ. He himself plainly acknowledges that without the aid of two Japanese gentlemen "the accompanying translation would have been impossible." We can only wonder, then, that with their help it should have been so excessively bad. It is not merely a question of downright blunders, from which none can hope to be wholly exempt. Omissions were frequent; hard passages were wilfully distorted or slurred over. Such offences are less pardonable. They would not be tolerated in any edition of a Greek or Latin classic, and a similar standard of honesty ought to be insisted upon in translations from Chinese.

From blemishes of this nature, at least, I believe that the present translation is free. It was not undertaken out of any inflated estimate of my own powers; but I could not help feeling that Sun Tzŭ deserved a better fate than had befallen him, and I knew that, at any rate, I could hardly fail to improve on the work of my predecessors. Towards the end of 1908, a new and revised edition of Capt. Calthrop's translation was published in London, this time, however, without any allusion to his Japanese collaborators. My first three chapters were then already in the printer's hands, so that the criticisms of Capt. Calthrop therein contained must be understood as referring to his earlier edition. This is on the whole an improvement on the other, thought there still remains much that cannot pass muster. Some of the grosser blunders have been rectified and lacunae filled up, but on the other hand a certain number of new mistakes appear. The very first sentence of the introduction is startlingly inaccurate; and later on, while mention is made of "an army of Japanese commentators" on Sun Tzŭ (who are these, by the way?), not a word is vouchsafed about the Chinese commentators, who nevertheless, I venture to assert, form a much more numerous and infinitely more important "army."

A few special features of the present volume may now be noticed. In the first place, the text has been cut up into numbered paragraphs, both in order to facilitate cross-reference and for the convenience of students generally. The division follows broadly that of Sun Hsing-yen's edition; but I have sometimes found it desirable to join two or more of his paragraphs into one. In quoting from other works, Chinese writers seldom give more than the bare title by way of reference, and the task of research is apt to be seriously hampered in consequence. With a view to obviating this difficulty so far as Sun Tzŭ is concerned, I have also appended a complete concordance of Chinese characters, following in this the admirable example of Legge, though an alphabetical arrangement has been preferred to the distribution under radicals which he adopted. Another feature borrowed from "The Chinese Classics" is the printing of text, translation and notes on the same page; the notes, however, are inserted, according to the Chinese method, immediately after the passages to which they refer. From the mass of native commentary my aim has been to extract the cream only, adding the Chinese text here and there when it seemed to present points of literary interest. Though constituting in itself an important branch of Chinese literature, very little commentary of this kind has hitherto been made directly accessible by translation.

I may say in conclusion that, owing to the printing off of my sheets as they were completed, the work has not had the benefit of a final revision. On a review of the whole, without modifying the substance of my criticisms, I might have been inclined in a few instances to temper their asperity. Having chosen to wield a bludgeon, however, I shall not cry out if in return I am visited with more than a rap over the knuckles. Indeed, I have been at some pains to put a sword into the hands of future opponents by scrupulously giving either text or reference for every passage translated. A scathing review, even from the pen of the Shanghai critic who despises "mere translations," would not, I must confess, be altogether unwelcome. For, after all, the worst fate I shall have to dread is that which befell the ingenious paradoxes of George in *The Vicar of Wakefield*.

Introduction

Sun Wu and his Book

Ssu-ma Ch'ien gives the following biography of Sun Tzŭ:[1]

> Sun Tzŭ Wu was a native of the Ch'i State. His *Art of War* brought him to the notice of Ho Lu,[2] King of Wu. Ho Lu said to him:
>
> "I have carefully perused your 13 chapters. May I submit your theory of managing soldiers to a slight test?"
>
> Sun Tzŭ replied: "You may."
>
> Ho Lu asked: "May the test be applied to women?"
>
> The answer was again in the affirmative, so arrangements were made to bring 180 ladies out of the Palace. Sun Tzŭ divided them into two companies, and placed one of the King's favourite concubines at the head of each. He then bade them all take spears in their hands, and addressed them thus: "I presume you know the difference between front and back, right hand and left hand?"
>
> The girls replied: Yes.

---

1. *Shih Chi*, ch. 65.

2. He reigned from 514 to 496 B.C.

Sun Tzŭ went on: "When I say "Eyes front," you must look straight ahead. When I say "Left turn," you must face towards your left hand. When I say "Right turn," you must face towards your right hand. When I say "About turn," you must face right round towards your back."

Again the girls assented. The words of command having been thus explained, he set up the halberds and battle-axes in order to begin the drill. Then, to the sound of drums, he gave the order "Right turn." But the girls only burst out laughing. Sun Tzŭ said: "If words of command are not clear and distinct, if orders are not thoroughly understood, then the general is to blame."

So he started drilling them again, and this time gave the order "Left turn," whereupon the girls once more burst into fits of laughter. Sun Tzŭ: "If words of command are not clear and distinct, if orders are not thoroughly understood, the general is to blame. But if his orders *are* clear, and the soldiers nevertheless disobey, then it is the fault of their officers."

So saying, he ordered the leaders of the two companies to be beheaded. Now the king of Wu was watching the scene from the top of a raised pavilion; and when he saw that his favourite concubines were about to be executed, he was greatly alarmed and hurriedly sent down the following message: "We are now quite satisfied as to our general's ability to handle troops. If we are bereft of these two concubines, our meat and drink will lose their savor. It is our wish that they shall not be beheaded."

Sun Tzŭ replied: "Having once received His Majesty's commission to be the general of his forces, there are certain commands of His Majesty which, acting in that capacity, I am unable to accept."

Accordingly, he had the two leaders beheaded, and straightway installed the pair next in order as leaders in their place. When this had been done, the drum was sounded for the drill once more; and the girls went through all the evolutions, turning to the right or to the left, marching ahead or wheeling back, kneeling or standing, with perfect accuracy and precision, not venturing to

> utter a sound. Then Sun Tzŭ sent a messenger to the King saying: "Your soldiers, Sire, are now properly drilled and disciplined, and ready for your majesty's inspection. They can be put to any use that their sovereign may desire; bid them go through fire and water, and they will not disobey."
>
> But the King replied: "Let our general cease drilling and return to camp. As for us, We have no wish to come down and inspect the troops."
>
> Thereupon Sun Tzŭ said: "The King is only fond of words, and cannot translate them into deeds."
>
> After that, Ho Lu saw that Sun Tzŭ was one who knew how to handle an army, and finally appointed him general. In the west, he defeated the Ch'u State and forced his way into Ying, the capital; to the north he put fear into the States of Ch'i and Chin, and spread his fame abroad amongst the feudal princes. And Sun Tzŭ shared in the might of the King.

About Sun Tzŭ himself this is all that Ssu-ma Ch'ien has to tell us in this chapter. But he proceeds to give a biography of his descendant, Sun Pin, born about a hundred years after his famous ancestor's death, and also the outstanding military genius of his time. The historian speaks of him too as Sun Tzŭ, and in his preface we read: "Sun Tzŭ had his feet cut off and yet continued to discuss the art of war."[3] It seems likely, then, that "Pin" was a nickname bestowed on him after his mutilation, unless the story was invented in order to account for the name. The crowning incident of his career, the crushing defeat of his treacherous rival P'ang Chuan, will be found briefly related in Chapter V. § 19, note.

To return to the elder Sun Tzŭ. He is mentioned in two other passages of the *Shih Chi*:—

> In the third year of his reign [512 B.C.] Ho Lu, king of Wu, took the field with Tzŭ-hsu [i.e. Wu Yuan] and Po P'ei, and

3. *Shih Chi*, ch. 130.

> attacked Ch'u. He captured the town of Shu and slew the two prince's sons who had formerly been generals of Wu. He was then meditating a descent on Ying [the capital]; but the general Sun Wu said: "The army is exhausted. It is not yet possible. We must wait".... [After further successful fighting,] "in the ninth year [506 B.C.], King Ho Lu addressed Wu Tzŭ-hsu and Sun Wu, saying: "Formerly, you declared that it was not yet possible for us to enter Ying. Is the time ripe now?" The two men replied: "Ch'u's general Tzŭ-ch'ang,[4] is grasping and covetous, and the princes of T'ang and Ts'ai both have a grudge against him. If Your Majesty has resolved to make a grand attack, you must win over T'ang and Ts'ai, and then you may succeed." Ho Lu followed this advice, [beat Ch'u in five pitched battles and marched into Ying.][5]

This is the latest date at which anything is recorded of Sun Wu. He does not appear to have survived his patron, who died from the effects of a wound in 496. In another chapter there occurs this passage:[6]

> From this time onward, a number of famous soldiers arose, one after the other: Kao-fan,[7] who was employed by the Chin State; Wang-tzu,[8] in the service of Ch'i; and Sun Wu, in the service of Wu. These men developed and threw light upon the principles of war.

It is obvious enough that Ssu-ma Ch'ien at least had no doubt about the reality of Sun Wu as an historical personage; and with one exception, to be noticed presently, he is by far the most important

---

4. The appellation of Nang Wa.

5. *Shih Chi*, ch. 31.

6. *Shih Chi*, ch. 25.

7. The appellation of Hu Yen, mentioned in ch. 39 under the year 637.

8. Wang-tzu Ch'eng-fu, ch. 32, year 607.

authority on the period in question. It will not be necessary, therefore, to say much of such a work as the *Wu Yüeh Ch'un Ch'iu*, which is supposed to have been written by Chao Yeh of the 1st century A.D. The attribution is somewhat doubtful; but even if it were otherwise, his account would be of little value, based as it is on the *Shih Chi* and expanded with romantic details. The story of Sun Tzŭ will be found, for what it is worth, in chapter 2. The only new points in it worth noting are: (1) Sun Tzŭ was first recommended to Ho Lu by Wu Tzŭ-hsu. (2) He is called a native of Wu. (3) He had previously lived a retired life, and his contemporaries were unaware of his ability.

The following passage occurs in the Huai-nan Tzŭ: "When sovereign and ministers show perversity of mind, it is impossible even for a Sun Tzŭ to encounter the foe." Assuming that this work is genuine (and hitherto no doubt has been cast upon it), we have here the earliest direct reference for Sun Tzŭ, for Huai-nan Tzŭ died in 122 B.C., many years before the *Shih Chi* was given to the world.

Liu Hsiang (80-9 B.C.) says: "The reason why Sun Tzŭ at the head of 30,000 men beat Ch'u with 200,000 is that the latter were undisciplined."

Teng Ming-shih informs us that the surname "Sun" was bestowed on Sun Wu's grandfather by Duke Ching of Ch'i [547-490 B.C.]. Sun Wu's father Sun P'ing, rose to be a Minister of State in Ch'i, and Sun Wu himself, whose style was Ch'ang-ch'ing, fled to Wu on account of the rebellion which was being fomented by the kindred of T'ien Pao. He had three sons, of whom the second, named Ming, was the father of Sun Pin. According to this account then, Pin was the grandson of Wu, which, considering that Sun Pin's victory over Wei was gained in 341 B.C., may be dismissed as chronologically impossible. Whence these data were obtained by Teng Ming-shih I do not know, but of course no reliance whatever can be placed in them.

An interesting document which has survived from the close of the Han period is the short preface written by the Great Ts'ao Ts'ao, or Wei Wu Ti, for his edition of Sun Tzŭ. I shall give it in full:—

I have heard that the ancients used bows and arrows to their advantage.[9] The *Lun Yu* says: "There must be a sufficiency of military strength." The *Shu Ching* mentions "the army" among the "eight objects of government." The *I Ching* says: "'army' indicates firmness and justice; the experienced leader will have good fortune." The *Shih Ching* says: "The King rose majestic in his wrath, and he marshalled his troops." The Yellow Emperor, T'ang the Completer and Wu Wang all used spears and battle-axes in order to succour their generation. The *Ssu-ma Fa* says: "If one man slay another of set purpose, he himself may rightfully be slain." He who relies solely on warlike measures shall be exterminated; he who relies solely on peaceful measures shall perish. Instances of this are Fu Ch'ai[10] on the one hand and Yen Wang on the other.[11] In military matters, the Sage's rule is normally to keep the peace, and to move his forces only when occasion requires. He will not use armed force unless driven to it by necessity.

Many books have I read on the subject of war and fighting; but the work composed by Sun Wu is the profoundest of them all. [Sun Tzŭ was a native of the Ch'i state, his personal name was Wu. He wrote the *Art of War* in 13 chapters for Ho Lu, King of Wu. Its principles were tested on women, and he was subsequently made a general. He led an army westwards, crushed the Ch'u state and entered Ying the capital. In the north, he kept Ch'i and Chin in awe. A hundred years and more after his time, Sun Pin lived. He was a descendant of Wu.][12] In his treatment of

---

9. "They attached strings to wood to make bows, and sharpened wood to make arrows. The use of bows and arrows is to keep the Empire in awe."

10. The son and successor of Ho Lu. He was finally defeated and overthrown by Kou chien, King of Yüeh, in 473 B.C. See post.

11. King Yen of Hsu, a fabulous being, of whom Sun Hsing-yen says in his preface: "His humanity brought him to destruction."

12. The passage I have put in brackets is omitted in the *T'u Shu*, and may be an interpolation. It was known, however to Chang Shou-chieh of the T'ang dynasty, and appears in the *T'ai P'ing Yu Lan*.

> deliberation and planning, the importance of rapidity in taking the field,[13] clearness of conception, and depth of design, Sun Tzŭ stands beyond the reach of carping criticism. My contemporaries, however, have failed to grasp the full meaning of his instructions, and while putting into practice the smaller details in which his work abounds, they have overlooked its essential purport. That is the motive which has led me to outline a rough explanation of the whole.

One thing to be noticed in the above is the explicit statement that the 13 chapters were specially composed for King Ho Lu. This is supported by the internal evidence of I. § 15, in which it seems clear that some ruler is addressed.

In the bibliographic section of the *Han Shu*, there is an entry which has given rise to much discussion: "The works of Sun Tzŭ of Wu in 82 *p'ien* (or chapters), with diagrams in 9 *chuan*." It is evident that this cannot be merely the 13 chapters known to Ssu-ma Ch'ien, or those we possess today. Chang Shou-chieh refers to an edition of Sun Tzŭ's *Art of War* of which the "13 chapters" formed the first *chuan*, adding that there were two other *chuan* besides. This has brought forth a theory, that the bulk of these 82 chapters consisted of other writings of Sun Tzŭ—we should call them apocryphal—similar to the *Wen Ta*, of which a specimen dealing with the Nine Situations[14] is preserved in the *T'ung Tien*, and another in Ho Shin's commentary. It is suggested that before his interview with Ho Lu, Sun Tzŭ had only written the 13 chapters, but afterwards composed a sort of exegesis in the form of question and answer between himself and the King. Pi I-hsun, the author of the *Sun Tzŭ Hsu Lu*, backs this up with a quotation from the *Wu Yüeh Ch'un Ch'iu:* "The King of Wu summoned Sun Tzŭ, and asked him questions about the art of war. Each time he set forth a chapter of his work, the King could not find words enough to praise him." As he

13. Ts'ao Kung seems to be thinking of the first part of chap. II, perhaps especially of § 8.

14. See chap. XI.

points out, if the whole work was expounded on the same scale as in the above-mentioned fragments, the total number of chapters could not fail to be considerable. Then the numerous other treatises attributed to Sun Tzŭ might be included. The fact that the *Han Chih* mentions no work of Sun Tzŭ except the 82 *p'ien*, whereas the Sui and T'ang bibliographies give the titles of others in addition to the "13 chapters," is good proof, Pi I-hsun thinks, that all of these were contained in the 82 *p'ien*. Without pinning our faith to the accuracy of details supplied by the *Wu Yüeh Ch'un Ch'iu*, or admitting the genuineness of any of the treatises cited by Pi I-hsun, we may see in this theory a probable solution of the mystery. Between Ssu-ma Ch'ien and Pan Ku there was plenty of time for a luxuriant crop of forgeries to have grown up under the magic name of Sun Tzŭ, and the 82 *p'ien* may very well represent a collected edition of these lumped together with the original work. It is also possible, though less likely, that some of them existed in the time of the earlier historian and were purposely ignored by him.[15]

Tu Mu's conjecture seems to be based on a passage which states: "Wei Wu Ti strung together Sun Wu's *Art of War*," which in turn may have resulted from a misunderstanding of the final words of Ts'ao King's preface. This, as Sun Hsing-yen points out, is only a modest way of saying that he made an explanatory paraphrase, or in other words, wrote a commentary on it. On the whole, this theory has met with very little acceptance. Thus, the *Ssu K'u Ch'uan Shu* says: "The mention of the 13 chapters in the *Shih Chi* shows that they were in existence before the *Han Chih*, and that latter accretions are not to be considered part of the original work. Tu Mu's assertion can certainly not be taken as proof."

There is every reason to suppose, then, that the 13 chapters existed in the time of Ssu-ma Ch'ien practically as we have

15. On the other hand, it is noteworthy that *Wu Tzŭ*, which is not in 6 chapters, has 48 assigned to it in the *Han Chih*. Likewise, the *Chung Yung* is credited with 49 chapters, though now only in one only. In the case of very short works, one is tempted to think that *p'ien* might simply mean "leaves."

them now. That the work was then well known he tells us in so many words. "Sun Tzŭ's *13 Chapters* and Wu Ch'i's *Art of War* are the two books that people commonly refer to on the subject of military matters. Both of them are widely distributed, so I will not discuss them here." But as we go further back, serious difficulties begin to arise. The salient fact which has to be faced is that the *Tso Chuan*, the greatest contemporary record, makes no mention whatsoever of Sun Wu, either as a general or as a writer. It is natural, in view of this awkward circumstance, that many scholars should not only cast doubt on the story of Sun Wu as given in the *Shih Chi*, but even show themselves frankly skeptical as to the existence of the man at all. The most powerful presentment of this side of the case is to be found in the following disposition by Yeh Shui-hsin:[16]—

> It is stated in Ssu-ma Ch'ien's history that Sun Wu was a native of the Ch'i State, and employed by Wu; and that in the reign of Ho Lu he crushed Ch'u, entered Ying, and was a great general. But in Tso's Commentary no Sun Wu appears at all. It is true that Tso's Commentary need not contain absolutely everything that other histories contain. But Tso has not omitted to mention vulgar plebeians and hireling ruffians such as Ying K'ao-shu,[17] Ts'ao Kuei,[18] Chu Chih-wu and Chuan She-chu[19] In the case of Sun Wu, whose fame and achievements were so brilliant, the omission is much more glaring. Again, details are given, in their due order, about his contemporaries Wu Yuan and the Minister P'ei.[20] Is it credible that Sun Wu alone should have been passed over?

---

16. Yeh Shih of the Sung dynasty [1151-1223].

17. He hardly deserves to be bracketed with assassins.

18. See Chapter 7, § 27 and Chapter 11, § 28.

19. See Chapter 11, § 28. Chuan Chu is the abbreviated form of his name.

20. I.e. Po P'ei. See ante.

In point of literary style, Sun Tzŭ's work belongs to the same school as *Kuan Tzŭ*,[21] *Liu T'ao*,[22] and the *Yüeh Yu*[23] and may have been the production of some private scholar living towards the end of the "Spring and Autumn" or the beginning of the "Warring States" period.[24] The story that his precepts were actually applied by the Wu State, is merely the outcome of big talk on the part of his followers.

From the flourishing period of the Chou dynasty25 down to the time of the "Spring and Autumn," all military commanders were statesmen as well, and the class of professional generals, for conducting external campaigns, did not then exist. It was not until the period of the "Six States"26 that this custom changed. Now although Wu was an uncivilized State, it is conceivable that Tso should have left unrecorded the fact that Sun Wu was a great general and yet held no civil office? What we are told, therefore, about Jang-chu27 and Sun Wu, is not authentic matter, but the reckless fabrication of theorizing pundits. The story of Ho Lu's experiment on the women, in particular, is utterly preposterous and incredible.

Yeh Shui-hsin represents Ssu-ma Ch'ien as having said that Sun Wu crushed Ch'u and entered Ying. This is not quite correct. No

---

21. The nucleus of this work is probably genuine, though large additions have been made by later hands. Kuan chung died in 645 B.C.

22. See infra, beginning of INTRODUCTION.

23. I do not know what this work, unless it be the last chapter of another work. Why that chapter should be singled out, however, is not clear.

24. About 480 B.C.

25. That is, I suppose, the age of Wu Wang and Chou Kung.

26. In the 3rd century B.C.

27. Ssu-ma Jang-chu, whose family name was T'ien, lived in the latter half of the 6th century B.C., and is also believed to have written a work on war. See *Shih Chi*, ch. 64, and infra at the beginning of the INTRODUCTION.

doubt the impression left on the reader's mind is that he at least shared in these exploits. The fact may or may not be significant; but it is nowhere explicitly stated in the *Shih Chi* either that Sun Tzŭ was general on the occasion of the taking of Ying, or that he even went there at all. Moreover, as we know that Wu Yuan and Po P'ei both took part in the expedition, and also that its success was largely due to the dash and enterprise of Fu Kai, Ho Lu's younger brother, it is not easy to see how yet another general could have played a very prominent part in the same campaign.

Ch'en Chen-sun of the Sung dynasty has the note:—

> Military writers look upon Sun Wu as the father of their art. But the fact that he does not appear in the *Tso Chuan*, although he is said to have served under Ho Lu King of Wu, makes it uncertain what period he really belonged to.

He also says:—

> The works of Sun Wu and Wu Ch'i may be of genuine antiquity.

It is noticeable that both Yeh Shui-hsin and Ch'en Chen-sun, while rejecting the personality of Sun Wu as he figures in Ssu-ma Ch'ien's history, are inclined to accept the date traditionally assigned to the work which passes under his name. The author of the *Hsu Lu* fails to appreciate this distinction, and consequently his bitter attack on Ch'en Chen-sun really misses its mark. He makes one of two points, however, which certainly tell in favour of the high antiquity of our "13 chapters." "Sun Tzŭ," he says, "must have lived in the age of Ching Wang [519-476], because he is frequently plagiarized in subsequent works of the Chou, Ch'in and Han dynasties." The two most shameless offenders in this respect are Wu Ch'i and Huai-nan Tzŭ, both of them important historical personages in their day. The former lived only a century after the alleged date of Sun Tzŭ, and his death is known to have taken place in 381 B.C. It was to him, according to Liu Hsiang, that Tseng Shen delivered the *Tso Chuan*, which had been entrusted to him by its author.[28] Now the fact that quotations from the *Art of War*, acknowledged or otherwise, are to be found in so many authors of different epochs, establishes a very strong anterior to them all,—in other words, that Sun Tzŭ's treatise was already in existence towards the end of the 5th century B.C. Further proof of Sun Tzŭ's antiquity is furnished by the archaic or wholly obsolete meanings attaching to a number of the words he uses. A list of these, which might perhaps be extended, is given in the *Hsu Lu;* and though some of the interpretations are doubtful, the main argument is hardly affected thereby. Again, it must not be forgotten that Yeh Shui-hsin, a scholar and critic of the first rank, deliberately pronounces the style of the 13 chapters to belong to the early part of the fifth century. Seeing that he is actually engaged in an attempt to disprove the existence of Sun Wu himself, we may be sure that he would not have hesitated to assign the work to a later date had he not honestly believed the contrary. And it is precisely on such a point that the judgment of an educated Chinaman will carry most weight. Other internal evidence is not far to seek. Thus in XIII. § 1, there is an unmistakable allusion to the ancient system of land-tenure which had already passed away by the time of Mencius, who was anxious to see it revived in a modified form.[29] The only warfare Sun Tzŭ knows is that carried on between the various feudal princes, in which armored chariots play a large part. Their use seems to have entirely died out before the end of the Chou dynasty. He speaks as a man of Wu, a state which ceased to exist as early as 473 B.C. On this I shall touch presently.

But once refer the work to the 5th century or earlier, and the chances of its being other than a *bonâ fide* production are sensibly diminished. The great age of forgeries did not come until long after. That it should have been forged in the period immediately following

---

28. See Legge's Classics, vol. V, Prolegomena p. 27. Legge thinks that the *Tso Chuan* must have been written in the 5th century, but not before 424 B.C.

29. See *Mencius* III. 1. iii. 13-20.

473 is particularly unlikely, for no one, as a rule, hastens to identify himself with a lost cause. As for Yeh Shui-hsin's theory, that the author was a literary recluse, that seems to me quite untenable. If one thing is more apparent than another after reading the maxims of Sun Tzŭ, it is that their essence has been distilled from a large store of personal observation and experience. They reflect the mind not only of a born strategist, gifted with a rare faculty of generalization, but also of a practical soldier closely acquainted with the military conditions of his time. To say nothing of the fact that these sayings have been accepted and endorsed by all the greatest captains of Chinese history, they offer a combination of freshness and sincerity, acuteness and common sense, which quite excludes the idea that they were artificially concocted in the study. If we admit, then, that the 13 chapters were the genuine production of a military man living towards the end of the "*Ch'un Ch'iu*" period, are we not bound, in spite of the silence of the *Tso Chuan*, to accept Ssu-ma Ch'ien's account in its entirety? In view of his high repute as a sober historian, must we not hesitate to assume that the records he drew upon for Sun Wu's biography were false and untrustworthy? The answer, I fear, must be in the negative. There is still one grave, if not fatal, objection to the chronology involved in the story as told in the *Shih Chi*, which, so far as I am aware, nobody has yet pointed out. There are two passages in Sun Tzŭ in which he alludes to contemporary affairs. The first in in VI. § 21:—

> Though according to my estimate the soldiers of Yüeh exceed our own in number, that shall advantage them nothing in the matter of victory. I say then that victory can be achieved.

The other is in XI. § 30:—

> Asked if an army can be made to imitate the *shuai-jan*, I should answer, Yes. For the men of Wu and the men of Yüeh are enemies; yet if they are crossing a river in the same boat and are caught by a storm, they will come to each other's assistance just as the left hand helps the right.

These two paragraphs are extremely valuable as evidence of the date of composition. They assign the work to the period of the struggle between Wu and Yüeh. So much has been observed by Pi I-hsun. But what has hitherto escaped notice is that they also seriously impair the credibility of Ssu-ma Ch'ien's narrative. As we have seen above, the first positive date given in connection with Sun Wu is 512 B.C. He is then spoken of as a general, acting as confidential adviser to Ho Lu, so that his alleged introduction to that monarch had already taken place, and of course the 13 chapters must have been written earlier still. But at that time, and for several years after, down to the capture of Ying in 506, Ch'u and not Yüeh, was the great hereditary enemy of Wu. The two states, Ch'u and Wu, had been constantly at war for over half a century,[30] whereas the first war between Wu and Yüeh was waged only in 510,[31] and even then was no more than a short interlude sandwiched in the midst of the fierce struggle with Ch'u. Now Ch'u is not mentioned in the 13 chapters at all. The natural inference is that they were written at a time when Yüeh had become the prime antagonist of Wu, that is, after Ch'u had suffered the great humiliation of 506. At this point, a table of dates may be found useful.

B.C.	
514	Accession of Ho Lu.
512	Ho Lu attacks Ch'u, but is dissuaded from entering Ying, the capital. *Shih Chi* mentions Sun Wu as general.
511	Another attack on Ch'u.
510	Wu makes a successful attack on Yüeh. This is the first war between the two states.

30. When Wu first appears in the *Ch'un Ch'iu* in 584, it is already at variance with its powerful neighbour. The *Ch'un Ch'iu* first mentions Yüeh in 537, the *Tso Chuan* in 601.

31. This is explicitly stated in the *Tso Chuan*, XXXII, 2.

509 or 508	Ch'u invades Wu, but is signally defeated at Yu-chang.
506	Ho Lu attacks Ch'u with the aid of T'ang and Ts'ai. Decisive battle of Po-chu, and capture of Ying. Last mention of Sun Wu in *Shih Chi*.
505	Yüeh makes a raid on Wu in the absence of its army. Wu is beaten by Ch'in and evacuates Ying.
504	Ho Lu sends Fu Ch'ai to attack Ch'u.
497	Kou Chien becomes King of Yüeh.
496	Wu attacks Yüeh, but is defeated by Kou Chien at Tsui-li. Ho Lu is killed.
494	Fu Ch'ai defeats Kou Chien in the great battle of Fu-chaio, and enters the capital of Yüeh.
485 or 484	Kou Chien renders homage to Wu. Death of Wu Tzŭ-hsu.
482	Kou Chien invades Wu in the absence of Fu Ch'ai.
478 to 476	Further attacks by Yüeh on Wu.
475	Kou Chien lays siege to the capital of Wu.
473	Final defeat and extinction of Wu.

The sentence quoted above from VI. § 21 hardly strikes me as one that could have been written in the full flush of victory. It seems rather to imply that, for the moment at least, the tide had turned against Wu, and that she was getting the worst of the struggle. Hence we may conclude that our treatise was not in existence in 505, before which date Yüeh does not appear to have scored any notable success against Wu. Ho Lu died in 496, so that if the book was written for him, it must have been during the period 505-496, when there was a lull in the hostilities, Wu having presumably exhausted by its supreme effort against Ch'u. On the other hand, if we choose to disregard the tradition connecting Sun Wu's name with Ho Lu, it might equally well have seen the light between 496 and 494, or possibly in the period 482-473, when Yüeh was once again becoming a very serious menace.[32] We may feel fairly certain that the author, whoever he may have been, was not a man of any great eminence in his own day. On this point the negative testimony of the *Tso Chuan* far outweighs any shred of authority still attaching to the *Shih Chi*, if once its other facts are discredited. Sun Hsing-yen, however, makes a feeble attempt to explain the omission of his name from the great commentary. It was Wu Tzŭ-hsu, he says, who got all the credit of Sun Wu's exploits, because the latter (being an alien) was not rewarded with an office in the State.

How then did the Sun Tzŭ legend originate? It may be that the growing celebrity of the book imparted by degrees a kind of factitious renown to its author. It was felt to be only right and proper that one so well versed in the science of war should have solid achievements to his credit as well. Now the capture of Ying was undoubtedly the greatest feat of arms in Ho Lu's reign; it made a deep and lasting impression on all the surrounding states, and raised Wu to the short-lived zenith of her power. Hence, what more natural, as time went on, than that the acknowledged master of strategy, Sun Wu, should be popularly identified with that campaign, at first perhaps only in the sense that his brain conceived and planned it; afterwards, that it was actually carried out by him in conjunction with Wu Yuan,[33] Po P'ei and Fu Kai?

It is obvious that any attempt to reconstruct even the outline of Sun Tzŭ's life must be based almost wholly on conjecture. With this necessary proviso, I should say that he probably entered the service of Wu about the time of Ho Lu's accession, and gathered experience, though only in the capacity of a subordinate officer,

---

32. There is this to be said for the later period, that the feud would tend to grow more bitter after each encounter, and thus more fully justify the language used in XI. § 30.

33. With Wu Yuan himself the case is just the reverse:—a spurious treatise on war has been fathered on him simply because he was a great general. Here we have an obvious inducement to forgery. Sun Wu, on the other hand, cannot have been widely known to fame in the 5th century.

during the intense military activity which marked the first half of the prince's reign.[34] If he rose to be a general at all, he certainly was never on an equal footing with the three above mentioned. He was doubtless present at the investment and occupation of Ying, and witnessed Wu's sudden collapse in the following year. Yüeh's attack at this critical juncture, when her rival was embarrassed on every side, seems to have convinced him that this upstart kingdom was the great enemy against whom every effort would henceforth have to be directed. Sun Wu was thus a well-seasoned warrior when he sat down to write his famous book, which according to my reckoning must have appeared towards the end, rather than the beginning of Ho Lu's reign. The story of the women may possibly have grown out of some real incident occurring about the same time. As we hear no more of Sun Wu after this from any source, he is hardly likely to have survived his patron or to have taken part in the death-struggle with Yüeh, which began with the disaster at Tsui-li.

If these inferences are approximately correct, there is a certain irony in the fate which decreed that China's most illustrious man of peace should be contemporary with her greatest writer on war.

The Text of Sun Tzŭ

I have found it difficult to glean much about the history of Sun Tzŭ's text. The quotations that occur in early authors go to show that the "13 chapters" of which Ssu-ma Ch'ien speaks were essentially the same as those now extant. We have his word for it that they were widely circulated in his day, and can only regret that he refrained from discussing them on that account. Sun Hsing-yen says in his preface:—

34. From *Tso Chuan:* "From the date of King Chao's accession [515] there was no year in which Ch'u was not attacked by Wu."

> During the Ch'in and Han dynasties Sun Tzŭ's *Art of War* was in general use amongst military commanders, but they seem to have treated it as a work of mysterious import, and were unwilling to expound it for the benefit of posterity. Thus it came about that Wei Wu was the first to write a commentary on it.

As we have already seen, there is no reasonable ground to suppose that Ts'ao Kung tampered with the text. But the text itself is often so obscure, and the number of editions which appeared from that time onward so great, especially during the T'ang and Sung dynasties, that it would be surprising if numerous corruptions had not managed to creep in. Towards the middle of the Sung period, by which time all the chief commentaries on Sun Tzŭ were in existence, a certain Chi T'ien-pao published a work in 15 *chuan* entitled "Sun Tzŭ with the collected commentaries of ten writers." There was another text, with variant readings put forward by Chu Fu of Ta-hsing, which also had supporters among the scholars of that period; but in the Ming editions, Sun Hsing-yen tells us, these readings were for some reason or other no longer put into circulation. Thus, until the end of the 18th century, the text in sole possession of the field was one derived from Chi T'ien-pao's edition, although no actual copy of that important work was known to have survived. That, therefore, is the text of Sun Tzŭ which appears in the War section of the great Imperial encyclopedia printed in 1726, the *Ku Chin T'u Shu Chi Ch'eng*. Another copy at my disposal of what is practically the same text, with slight variations, is that contained in the "Eleven philosophers of the Chou and Ch'in dynasties" [1758]. And the Chinese printed in Capt. Calthrop's first edition is evidently a similar version which has filtered through Japanese channels. So things remained until Sun Hsing-yen [1752-1818], a distinguished antiquarian and classical scholar, who claimed to be an actual descendant of Sun Wu,[35] accidentally discovered a copy of Chi

35. Preface ad fin: "My family comes from Lo-an, and we are really descended from Sun Tzŭ. I am ashamed to say that I only read my ancestor's work from a literary

T'ien-pao's long-lost work, when on a visit to the library of the Hua-yin temple.[36] Appended to it was the *I Shuo* of Cheng Yu-Hsien, mentioned in the *T'ung Chih*, and also believed to have perished. This is what Sun Hsing-yen designates as the "original edition (or text)"—a rather misleading name, for it cannot by any means claim to set before us the text of Sun Tzŭ in its pristine purity. Chi T'ien-pao was a careless compiler, and appears to have been content to reproduce the somewhat debased version current in his day, without troubling to collate it with the earliest editions then available. Fortunately, two versions of Sun Tzŭ, even older than the newly discovered work, were still extant, one buried in the *T'ung Tien*, Tu Yu's great treatise on the Constitution, the other similarly enshrined in the *T'ai P'ing Yu Lan* encyclopedia. In both the complete text is to be found, though split up into fragments, intermixed with other matter, and scattered piecemeal over a number of different sections. Considering that the *Yu Lan* takes us back to the year 983, and the *T'ung Tien* about 200 years further still, to the middle of the T'ang dynasty, the value of these early transcripts of Sun Tzŭ can hardly be overestimated. Yet the idea of utilizing them does not seem to have occurred to anyone until Sun Hsing-yen, acting under Government instructions, undertook a thorough recension of the text. This is his own account:—

> Because of the numerous mistakes in the text of Sun Tzŭ which his editors had handed down, the Government ordered that the ancient edition [of Chi T'ien-pao] should be used, and that the text should be revised and corrected throughout. It happened that

---

point of view, without comprehending the military technique. So long have we been enjoying the blessings of peace!"

36. Hoa-yin is about 14 miles from T'ung-kuan on the eastern border of Shensi. The temple in question is still visited by those about the ascent of the Western Sacred Mountain. It is mentioned in a text as being "situated five *li* east of the district city of Hua-yin. The temple contains the Hua-shan tablet inscribed by the T'ang Emperor Hsuan Tsung [713-755]."

> Wu Nien-hu, the Governor Pi Kua, and Hsi, a graduate of the second degree, had all devoted themselves to this study, probably surpassing me therein. Accordingly, I have had the whole work cut on blocks as a textbook for military men.

The three individuals here referred to had evidently been occupied on the text of Sun Tzŭ prior to Sun Hsing-yen's commission, but we are left in doubt as to the work they really accomplished. At any rate, the new edition, when ultimately produced, appeared in the names of Sun Hsing-yen and only one co-editor Wu Jen-shi. They took the "original edition" as their basis, and by careful comparison with older versions, as well as the extant commentaries and other sources of information such as the *I Shuo*, succeeded in restoring a very large number of doubtful passages, and turned out, on the whole, what must be accepted as the closest approximation we are ever likely to get to Sun Tzŭ's original work. This is what will hereafter be denominated the "standard text."

The copy which I have used belongs to a reissue dated 1877. It is in 6 *pen*, forming part of a well-printed set of 23 early philosophical works in 83 *pen*.[37] It opens with a preface by Sun Hsing-yen (largely quoted in this introduction), vindicating the traditional view of Sun Tzŭ's life and performances, and summing up in remarkably concise fashion the evidence in its favour. This is followed by Ts'ao Kung's preface to his edition, and the biography of Sun Tzŭ from the *Shih Chi*, both translated above. Then come, firstly, Cheng Yu-hsien's *I Shuo*,[38] with author's preface, and next, a short miscellany of historical and bibliographical information entitled *Sun Tzŭ Hsu Lu*, compiled by Pi I-hsun. As regards the body of the work, each separate sentence is followed by a note on the text, if required, and then by the various commentaries appertaining to it, arranged in chronological order. These we shall now proceed to discuss briefly, one by one.

---

37. See my "Catalogue of Chinese Books" (Luzac & Co., 1908), no. 40.

38. This is a discussion of 29 difficult passages in Sun Tzŭ.

The Commentators

Sun Tzŭ can boast an exceptionally long distinguished roll of commentators, which would do honour to any classic. Ou-yang Hsiu remarks on this fact, though he wrote before the tale was complete, and rather ingeniously explains it by saying that the artifices of war, being inexhaustible, must therefore be susceptible of treatment in a great variety of ways.

1. TS'AO TS'AO or Ts'ao Kung, afterwards known as Wei Wu Ti [A.D. 155-220]. There is hardly any room for doubt that the earliest commentary on Sun Tzŭ actually came from the pen of this extraordinary man, whose biography in the *San Kuo Chih* reads like a romance. One of the greatest military geniuses that the world has seen, and Napoleonic in the scale of his operations, he was especially famed for the marvelous rapidity of his marches, which has found expression in the line "Talk of Ts'ao Ts'ao, and Ts'ao Ts'ao will appear." Ou-yang Hsiu says of him that he was a great captain who "measured his strength against Tung Cho, Lu Pu and the two Yuan, father and son, and vanquished them all; whereupon he divided the Empire of Han with Wu and Shu, and made himself king. It is recorded that whenever a council of war was held by Wei on the eve of a far-reaching campaign, he had all his calculations ready; those generals who made use of them did not lose one battle in ten; those who ran counter to them in any particular saw their armies incontinently beaten and put to flight." Ts'ao Kung's notes on Sun Tzŭ, models of austere brevity, are so thoroughly characteristic of the stern commander known to history, that it is hard indeed to conceive of them as the work of a mere *littérateur*. Sometimes, indeed, owing to extreme compression, they are scarcely intelligible and stand no less in need of a commentary than the text itself.[39]

---

39. Cf. Catalogue of the library of Fan family at Ningpo: "His commentary is frequently obscure; it furnishes a clue, but does not fully develop the meaning."

2. MENG SHIH. The commentary which has come down to us under this name is comparatively meager, and nothing about the author is known. Even his personal name has not been recorded. Chi T'ien-pao's edition places him after Chia Lin, and Ch'ao Kung-wu also assigns him to the T'ang dynasty,[40] but this is a mistake. In Sun Hsing-yen's preface, he appears as Meng Shih of the Liang dynasty [502-557]. Others would identify him with Meng K'ang of the 3rd century. He is named in one work as the last of the "Five Commentators," the others being Wei Wu Ti, Tu Mu, Ch'en Hao and Chia Lin.

3. LI CH'UAN of the 8th century was a well-known writer on military tactics. One of his works has been in constant use down to the present day. The *T'ung Chih* mentions "Lives of famous generals from the Chou to the T'ang dynasty" as written by him.[41] According to Ch'ao Kung-wu and the *T'ien-i-ko* catalogue, he followed a variant of the text of Sun Tzŭ which differs considerably from those now extant. His notes are mostly short and to the point, and he frequently illustrates his remarks by anecdotes from Chinese history.

4. TU YU (died 812) did not publish a separate commentary on Sun Tzŭ, his notes being taken from the *T'ung Tien*, the encyclopedic treatise on the Constitution which was his life-work. They are largely repetitions of Ts'ao Kung and Meng Shih, besides which it is believed that he drew on the ancient commentaries of Wang Ling and others. Owing to the peculiar arrangement of *T'ung Tien*, he has to explain each passage on its merits, apart from the context, and sometimes his own explanation does not agree with that of Ts'ao Kung, whom he always quotes first. Though not strictly to be reckoned as one of the "Ten Commentators," he was added to their number by Chi T'ien-pao, being wrongly placed after his grandson Tu Mu.

---

40. *Wen Hsien T'ung K'ao*, ch. 221.

41. It is interesting to note that M. Pelliot has recently discovered chapters 1, 4 and 5 of this lost work in the "Grottos of the Thousand Buddhas." See B.E.F.E.O., t. VIII, nos. 3-4, p. 525.

5. TU MU (803-852) is perhaps the best known as a poet—a bright star even in the glorious galaxy of the T'ang period. We learn from Ch'ao Kung-wu that although he had no practical experience of war, he was extremely fond of discussing the subject, and was moreover well read in the military history of the *Ch'un Ch'iu* and *Chan Kuo* eras. His notes, therefore, are well worth attention. They are very copious, and replete with historical parallels. The gist of Sun Tzŭ's work is thus summarized by him: "Practice benevolence and justice, but on the other hand make full use of artifice and measures of expediency." He further declared that all the military triumphs and disasters of the thousand years which had elapsed since Sun Tzŭ's death would, upon examination, be found to uphold and corroborate, in every particular, the maxims contained in his book. Tu Mu's somewhat spiteful charge against Ts'ao Kung has already been considered elsewhere.

6. CH'EN HAO appears to have been a contemporary of Tu Mu. Ch'ao Kung-wu says that he was impelled to write a new commentary on Sun Tzŭ because Ts'ao Kung's on the one hand was too obscure and subtle, and that of Tu Mu on the other too long-winded and diffuse. Ou-yang Hsiu, writing in the middle of the 11th century, calls Ts'ao Kung, Tu Mu and Ch'en Hao the three chief commentators on Sun Tzŭ, and observes that Ch'en Hao is continually attacking Tu Mu's shortcomings. His commentary, though not lacking in merit, must rank below those of his predecessors.

7. CHIA LIN is known to have lived under the T'ang dynasty, for his commentary on Sun Tzŭ is mentioned in the *T'ang Shu* and was afterwards republished by Chi Hsieh of the same dynasty together with those of Meng Shih and Tu Yu. It is of somewhat scanty texture, and in point of quality, too, perhaps the least valuable of the eleven.

8. MEI YAO-CH'EN (1002-1060), commonly known by his "style" as Mei Sheng-yu, was, like Tu Mu, a poet of distinction. His commentary was published with a laudatory preface by the great Ou-yang Hsiu, from which we may cull the following:—

> Later scholars have misread Sun Tzŭ, distorting his words and trying to make them square with their own one-sided views. Thus, though commentators have not been lacking, only a few have proved equal to the task. My friend Sheng-yu has not fallen into this mistake. In attempting to provide a critical commentary for Sun Tzŭ's work, he does not lose sight of the fact that these sayings were intended for states engaged in internecine warfare; that the author is not concerned with the military conditions prevailing under the sovereigns of the three ancient dynasties,[42] nor with the nine punitive measures prescribed to the Minister of War.[43] Again, Sun Wu loved brevity of diction, but his meaning is always deep. Whether the subject be marching an army, or handling soldiers, or estimating the enemy, or controlling the forces of victory, it is always systematically treated; the sayings are bound together in strict logical sequence, though this has been obscured by commentators who have probably failed to grasp their meaning. In his own commentary, Mei Sheng-yu has brushed aside all the obstinate prejudices of these critics, and has tried to bring out the true meaning of Sun Tzŭ himself. In this way, the clouds of confusion have been dispersed and the sayings made clear. I am convinced that the present work deserves to be handed down side by side with the three great commentaries; and for a great deal that they find in the sayings, coming generations will have constant reason to thank my friend Sheng-yu.

Making some allowance for the exuberance of friendship, I am inclined to endorse this favourable judgment, and would certainly place him above Ch'en Hao in order of merit.

---

42. The Hsia, the Shang and the Chou. Although the last-named was nominally existent in Sun Tzŭ's day, it retained hardly a vestige of power, and the old military organization had practically gone by the board. I can suggest no other explanation of the passage.

43. See *Chou Li*, xxix. 6-10.

9. WANG HSI, also of the Sung dynasty, is decidedly original in some of his interpretations, but much less judicious than Mei Yao-ch'en, and on the whole not a very trustworthy guide. He is fond of comparing his own commentary with that of Ts'ao Kung, but the comparison is not often flattering to him. We learn from Ch'ao Kung-wu that Wang Hsi revised the ancient text of Sun Tzŭ, filling up lacunae and correcting mistakes.[44]

10. HO YEN-HSI of the Sung dynasty. The personal name of this commentator is given as above by Cheng Ch'iao in the *Tung Chih*, written about the middle of the twelfth century, but he appears simply as Ho Shih in the *Yu Hai*, and Ma Tuan-lin quotes Ch'ao Kung-wu as saying that his personal name is unknown. There seems to be no reason to doubt Cheng Ch'iao's statement, otherwise I should have been inclined to hazard a guess and identify him with one Ho Ch'u-fei, the author of a short treatise on war, who lived in the latter part of the 11th century. Ho Shih's commentary, in the words of the *T'ien-i-ko* catalogue, "contains helpful additions" here and there, but is chiefly remarkable for the copious extracts taken, in adapted form, from the dynastic histories and other sources.

11. CHANG YU. The list closes with a commentator of no great originality perhaps, but gifted with admirable powers of lucid exposition. His commentator is based on that of Ts'ao Kung, whose terse sentences he contrives to expand and develop in masterly fashion. Without Chang Yu, it is safe to say that much of Ts'ao Kung's commentary would have remained cloaked in its pristine obscurity and therefore valueless. His work is not mentioned in the Sung history, the *T'ung K'ao*, or the *Yu Hai*, but it finds a niche in the *T'ung Chih*, which also names him as the author of the "Lives of Famous Generals."[45]

---

44. *T'ung K'ao*, loc. cit.

45. This appears to be still extant. See Wylie's "Notes," p. 91 (new edition).

It is rather remarkable that the last-named four should all have flourished within so short a space of time. Ch'ao Kung-wu accounts for it by saying: "During the early years of the Sung dynasty the Empire enjoyed a long spell of peace, and men ceased to practice the art of war. But when [Chao] Yuan-hao's rebellion came [1038-42] and the frontier generals were defeated time after time, the Court made strenuous inquiry for men skilled in war, and military topics became the vogue amongst all the high officials. Hence it is that the commentators of Sun Tzŭ in our dynasty belong mainly to that period.[46]

Besides these eleven commentators, there are several others whose work has not come down to us. The *Sui Shu* mentions four, namely Wang Ling (often quoted by Tu Yu as Wang Tzŭ); Chang Tzŭ-shang; Chia Hsu of Wei;[47] and Shen Yu of Wu. The *T'ang Shu* adds Sun Hao, and the *T'ung Chih* Hsiao Chi, while the *T'u Shu* mentions a Ming commentator, Huang Jun-yu. It is possible that some of these may have been merely collectors and editors of other commentaries, like Chi T'ien-pao and Chi Hsieh, mentioned above.

Appreciations of Sun Tzŭ

Sun Tzŭ has exercised a potent fascination over the minds of some of China's greatest men. Among the famous generals who are known to have studied his pages with enthusiasm may be mentioned Han Hsin (*d.* 196 B.C.),[48] Feng I (*d.* 34 A.D.),[49] Lu Meng (*d.* 219),[50]

46. *T'ung K'ao*, loc. cit.

47. A notable person in his day. His biography is given in the *San Kuo Chih*, ch. 10.

48. See XI. § 58, note.

49. *Hou Han Shu*, ch. 17 ad init.

50. *San Kuo Chih*, ch. 54.

and Yo Fei (1103-1141). [51]The opinion of Ts'ao Kung, who disputes with Han Hsin the highest place in Chinese military annals, has already been recorded.[52] Still more remarkable, in one way, is the testimony of purely literary men, such as Su Hsun (the father of Su Tung-p'o), who wrote several essays on military topics, all of which owe their chief inspiration to Sun Tzŭ. The following short passage by him is preserved in the *Yu Hai*:[53]—

> Sun Wu's saying, that in war one cannot make certain of conquering,[54] is very different indeed from what other books tell us.[55] Wu Ch'i was a man of the same stamp as Sun Wu: they both wrote books on war, and they are linked together in popular speech as "Sun and Wu." But Wu Ch'i's remarks on war are less weighty, his rules are rougher and more crudely stated, and there is not the same unity of plan as in Sun Tzŭ's work, where the style is terse, but the meaning fully brought out.

The following is an extract from the "Impartial Judgments in the Garden of Literature" by Cheng Hou:—

> Sun Tzŭ's 13 chapters are not only the staple and base of all military men's training, but also compel the most careful attention of scholars and men of letters. His sayings are terse yet elegant, simple yet profound, perspicuous and eminently practical. Such

---

51. *Sung Shih*, ch. 365 ad init.

52. The few Europeans who have yet had an opportunity of acquainting themselves with Sun Tzŭ are not behindhand in their praise. In this connection, I may perhaps be excused for quoting from a letter from Lord Roberts, to whom the sheets of the present work were submitted previous to publication: "Many of Sun Wu's maxims are perfectly applicable to the present day, and no. 11 [in Chapter VIII] is one that the people of this country would do well to take to heart."

53. Ch. 140.

54. See IV. § 3.

55. The allusion may be to Mencius VI. 2. ix. 2.

works as the *Lun Yu*, the *I Ching* and the great Commentary,[56] as well as the writings of Mencius, Hsun K'uang and Yang Chu, all fall below the level of Sun Tzŭ.

Chu Hsi, commenting on this, fully admits the first part of the criticism, although he dislikes the audacious comparison with the venerated classical works. Language of this sort, he says, "encourages a ruler's bent towards unrelenting warfare and reckless militarism."

Apologies for War

Accustomed as we are to think of China as the greatest peace-loving nation on earth, we are in some danger of forgetting that her experience of war in all its phases has also been such as no modern State can parallel. Her long military annals stretch back to a point at which they are lost in the mists of time. She had built the Great Wall and was maintaining a huge standing army along her frontier centuries before the first Roman legionary was seen on the Danube. What with the perpetual collisions of the ancient feudal States, the grim conflicts with Huns, Turks and other invaders after the centralization of government, the terrific upheavals which accompanied the overthrow of so many dynasties, besides the countless rebellions and minor disturbances that have flamed up and flickered out again one by one, it is hardly too much to say that the clash of arms has never ceased to resound in one portion or another of the Empire.

No less remarkable is the succession of illustrious captains to whom China can point with pride. As in all countries, the greatest are fond of emerging at the most fateful crises of her history. Thus, Po Ch'i stands out conspicuous in the period when Ch'in was entering upon her final struggle with the remaining independent states. The

56. The *Tso Chuan*.

stormy years which followed the break-up of the Ch'in dynasty are illuminated by the transcendent genius of Han Hsin. When the House of Han in turn is tottering to its fall, the great and baleful figure of Ts'ao Ts'ao dominates the scene. And in the establishment of the T'ang dynasty, one of the mightiest tasks achieved by man, the superhuman energy of Li Shih-min (afterwards the Emperor T'ai Tsung) was seconded by the brilliant strategy of Li Ching. None of these generals need fear comparison with the greatest names in the military history of Europe.

In spite of all this, the great body of Chinese sentiment, from Lao Tzŭ downwards, and especially as reflected in the standard literature of Confucianism, has been consistently pacific and intensely opposed to militarism in any form. It is such an uncommon thing to find any of the literati defending warfare on principle, that I have thought it worth while to collect and translate a few passages in which the unorthodox view is upheld. The following, by Ssu-ma Ch'ien, shows that for all his ardent admiration of Confucius, he was yet no advocate of peace at any price:—

> Military weapons are the means used by the Sage to punish violence and cruelty, to give peace to troublous times, to remove difficulties and dangers, and to succour those who are in peril. Every animal with blood in its veins and horns on its head will fight when it is attacked. How much more so will man, who carries in his breast the faculties of love and hatred, joy and anger! When he is pleased, a feeling of affection springs up within him; when angry, his poisoned sting is brought into play. That is the natural law which governs his being.... What then shall be said of those scholars of our time, blind to all great issues, and without any appreciation of relative values, who can only bark out their stale formulas about "virtue" and "civilization," condemning the use of military weapons? They will surely bring our country to impotence and dishonour and the loss of her rightful heritage; or, at the very least, they will bring about invasion and rebellion, sacrifice of territory and general enfeeblement. Yet they obstinately

> refuse to modify the position they have taken up. The truth is that, just as in the family the teacher must not spare the rod, and punishments cannot be dispensed with in the State, so military chastisement can never be allowed to fall into abeyance in the Empire. All one can say is that this power will be exercised wisely by some, foolishly by others, and that among those who bear arms some will be loyal and others rebellious.[57]

The next piece is taken from Tu Mu's preface to his commentary on Sun Tzŭ:—

> War may be defined as punishment, which is one of the functions of government. It was the profession of Chung Yu and Jan Ch'iu, both disciples of Confucius. Nowadays, the holding of trials and hearing of litigation, the imprisonment of offenders and their execution by flogging in the market-place, are all done by officials. But the wielding of huge armies, the throwing down of fortified cities, the hauling of women and children into captivity, and the beheading of traitors—this is also work which is done by officials. The objects of the rack and of military weapons are essentially the same. There is no intrinsic difference between the punishment of flogging and cutting off heads in war. For the lesser infractions of law, which are easily dealt with, only a small amount of force need be employed: hence the use of military weapons and wholesale decapitation. In both cases, however, the end in view is to get rid of wicked people, and to give comfort and relief to the good....
>
> Chi-sun asked Jan Yu, saying: "Have you, Sir, acquired your military aptitude by study, or is it innate?" Jan Yu replied: "It has been acquired by study."[58] "How can that be so," said Chi-sun, "seeing that you are a disciple of Confucius?" "It is a fact," replied Jan Yu; "I was taught by Confucius. It is fitting that the great Sage

57. *Shih Chi*, ch. 25, fol. I.

58. Cf. *Shih Chi*, ch 47.

should exercise both civil and military functions, though to be sure my instruction in the art of fighting has not yet gone very far."

Now, who the author was of this rigid distinction between the "civil" and the "military," and the limitation of each to a separate sphere of action, or in what year of which dynasty it was first introduced, is more than I can say. But, at any rate, it has come about that the members of the governing class are quite afraid of enlarging on military topics, or do so only in a shamefaced manner. If any are bold enough to discuss the subject, they are at once set down as eccentric individuals of coarse and brutal propensities. This is an extraordinary instance in which, through sheer lack of reasoning, men unhappily lose sight of fundamental principles.

When the Duke of Chou was minister under Ch'eng Wang, he regulated ceremonies and made music, and venerated the arts of scholarship and learning; yet when the barbarians of the River Huai revolted,[59] he sallied forth and chastised them. When Confucius held office under the Duke of Lu, and a meeting was convened at Chia-ku,[60] he said: "If pacific negotiations are in progress, warlike preparations should have been made beforehand." He rebuked and shamed the Marquis of Ch'i, who cowered under him and dared not proceed to violence. How can it be said that these two great Sages had no knowledge of military matters?

We have seen that the great Chu Hsi held Sun Tzŭ in high esteem. He also appeals to the authority of the Classics:—

Our Master Confucius, answering Duke Ling of Wei, said: "I have never studied matters connected with armies and battalions."[61] Replying to K'ung Wen-tzu, he said: I have not been instructed about buff-coats and weapons." But if we turn to the meeting at

59. See *Shu Ching*, preface § 55.

60. See *Shih Chi*, ch. 47.

61. *Lun Yu*, XV. 1.

> Chia-ku, we find that he used armed force against the men of Lai, so that the marquis of Ch'i was overawed. Again, when the inhabitants of Pi revolted; he ordered his officers to attack them, whereupon they were defeated and fled in confusion. He once uttered the words: "If I fight, I conquer."[62] And Jan Yu also said: "The Sage exercises both civil and military functions."[63] Can it be a fact that Confucius never studied or received instruction in the art of war? We can only say that he did not specially choose matters connected with armies and fighting to be the subject of his teaching.

Sun Hsing-yen, the editor of Sun Tzŭ, writes in similar strain:—

> Confucius said: "I am unversed in military matters."[64] He also said: "If I fight, I conquer." Confucius ordered ceremonies and regulated music. Now war constitutes one of the five classes of State ceremonial,[65] and must not be treated as an independent branch of study. Hence, the words "I am unversed in" must be taken to mean that there are things which even an inspired Teacher does not know. Those who have to lead an army and devise stratagems, must learn the art of war. But if one can command the services of a good general like Sun Tzŭ, who was employed by Wu Tzŭ-hsu, there is no need to learn it oneself. Hence the remark added by Confucius: "If I fight, I conquer."
>
> The men of the present day, however, willfully interpret these words of Confucius in their narrowest sense, as though he meant that books on the art of war were not worth reading. With blind persistency, they adduce the example of Chao Kua, who pored

62. I failed to trace this utterance.

63. Supra.

64. Supra.

65. The other four being worship, mourning, entertainment of guests, and festive rites. See *Shu Ching*, ii. 1. III. 8, and *Chou Li*, IX. fol. 49.

over his father's books to no purpose,[66] as a proof that all military theory is useless. Again, seeing that books on war have to do with such things as opportunism in designing plans, and the conversion of spies, they hold that the art is immoral and unworthy of a sage. These people ignore the fact that the studies of our scholars and the civil administration of our officials also require steady application and practice before efficiency is reached. The ancients were particularly chary of allowing mere novices to botch their work.[67] Weapons are baneful[68] and fighting perilous; and useless unless a general is in constant practice, he ought not to hazard other men's lives in battle.[69] Hence it is essential that Sun Tzŭ's 13 chapters should be studied.

Hsiang Liang used to instruct his nephew Chi[70] in the art of war. Chi got a rough idea of the art in its general bearings, but would not pursue his studies to their proper outcome, the consequence being that he was finally defeated and overthrown. He did not realize that the tricks and artifices of war are beyond verbal computation. Duke Hsiang of Sung and King Yen of Hsu were brought to destruction by their misplaced humanity. The treacherous and underhand nature of war necessitates the use of guile and stratagem suited to the occasion. There is a case on record of Confucius himself having violated an extorted oath,[71] and also of his having left the Sung State in disguise.[72] Can we then recklessly arraign Sun Tzŭ for disregarding truth and honesty?

66. See XIII. § 11, note.

67. This is a rather obscure allusion to the *Tso Chuan*, where Tzŭ-ch'an says: "If you have a piece of beautiful brocade, you will not employ a mere learner to make it up."

68. Cf. *Tao Te Ching*, ch. 31.

69. Sun Hsing-yen might have quoted Confucius again. See *Lun Yu*, XIII. 29, 30.

70. Better known as Hsiang Yu [233-202 B.C.].

71. *Shih Chi*, ch. 47.

72. *Shih Chi*, ch. 38.

Bibliography

The following are the oldest Chinese treatises on war, after Sun Tzŭ. The notes on each have been drawn principally from the *Ssu k'u ch'uan shu chien ming mu lu*, ch. 9, fol. 22 sqq.

1. *Wu Tzŭ*, in 1 *chuan* or 6 chapters. By Wu Ch'i (*d.* 381 B.C.). A genuine work. See *Shih Chi*, ch. 65.

2. *Ssu-ma Fa*, in 1 *chuan* or 5 chapters. Wrongly attributed to Ssu-ma Jang-chu of the 6th century B.C. Its date, however, must be early, as the customs of the three ancient dynasties are constantly to be met within its pages. See *Shih Chi*, ch. 64.

The *Ssu K'u Ch'uan Shu* (ch. 99, f. 1) remarks that the oldest three treatises on war, *Sun Tzŭ*, *Wu Tzŭ* and *Ssu-ma Fa*, are, generally speaking, only concerned with things strictly military—the art of producing, collecting, training and drilling troops, and the correct theory with regard to measures of expediency, laying plans, transport of goods and the handling of soldiers—in strong contrast to later works, in which the science of war is usually blended with metaphysics, divination and magical arts in general.

3. *Liu T'ao*, in 6 *chuan*, or 60 chapters. Attributed to Lu Wang (or Lu Shang, also known as T'ai Kung) of the 12th century B.C.[73] But its style does not belong to the era of the Three Dynasties. Lu Te-ming (550-625 A.D.) mentions the work, and enumerates the headings of the six sections so that the forgery cannot have been later than Sui dynasty.

4. *Wei Liao Tzŭ*, in 5 *chuan*. Attributed to Wei Liao (4th cent. B.C.), who studied under the famous Kuei-ku Tzŭ. The work appears to

---

73. See XIII. § 27, note. Further details on T'ai Kung will be found in the *Shih Chi*, ch. 32 ad init. Besides the tradition which makes him a former minister of Chou Hsin, two other accounts of him are there given, according to which he would appear to have been first raised from a humble private station by Wen Wang.

have been originally in 31 chapters, whereas the text we possess contains only 24. Its matter is sound enough in the main, though the strategical devices differ considerably from those of the Warring States period. It is been furnished with a commentary by the well-known Sung philosopher Chang Tsai.

5. *San Lueh* in 3 *chuan*. Attributed to Huang-shih Kung, a legendary personage who is said to have bestowed it on Chang Liang (*d.* 187 B.C.) in an interview on a bridge. But here again, the style is not that of works dating from the Ch'in or Han period. The Han Emperor Kuang Wu [25-57 A.D.] apparently quotes from it in one of his proclamations; but the passage in question may have been inserted later on, in order to prove the genuineness of the work. We shall not be far out if we refer it to the Northern Sung period [420-478 A.D.], or somewhat earlier.

6. *Li Wei Kung Wen Tui*, in 3 sections. Written in the form of a dialogue between T'ai Tsung and his great general Li Ching, it is usually ascribed to the latter. Competent authorities consider it a forgery, though the author was evidently well versed in the art of war.

7. *Li Ching Ping Fa* (not to be confounded with the foregoing) is a short treatise in 8 chapters, preserved in the T'ung Tien, but not published separately. This fact explains its omission from the *Ssu K'u Ch'uan Shu*.

8. *Wu Ch'i Ching*, in 1 *chuan*. Attributed to the legendary minister Feng Hou, with exegetical notes by Kung-sun Hung of the Han dynasty (*d.* 121 B.C.), and said to have been eulogized by the celebrated general Ma Lung (*d.* 300 A.D.). Yet the earliest mention of it is in the *Sung Chih*. Although a forgery, the work is well put together.

Considering the high popular estimation in which Chu-ko Liang has always been held, it is not surprising to find more than one work on war ascribed to his pen. Such are (1) the *Shih Liu Ts'e* (1 *chuan*), preserved in the *Yung Lo Ta Tien;* (2) *Chiang Yuan* (1 *chuan*); and (3)

Hsin Shu (1 *chuan*), which steals wholesale from Sun Tzŭ. None of these has the slightest claim to be considered genuine.

Most of the large Chinese encyclopedias contain extensive sections devoted to the literature of war. The following references may be found useful:—

T'ung Tien (circa 800 A.D.), ch. 148-162.

T'ai P'ing Yu Lan (983), ch. 270-359.

Wen Hsien Tung K'ao (13th cent.), ch. 221.

Yu Hai (13th cent.), ch. 140, 141.

San Ts'ai T'u Hui (16th cent).

Kuang Po Wu Chih (1607), ch. 31, 32. *Ch'ien Ch'io Lei Shu* (1632), ch. 75. *Yuan Chien Lei Han* (1710), ch. 206-229.

Ku Chin T'u Shu Chi Ch'eng (1726), section XXX, esp. ch. 81-90.

Hsu Wen Hsien T'ung K'ao (1784), ch. 121-134.

Huang Ch'ao Ching Shih Wen Pien (1826), ch. 76, 77.

The bibliographical sections of certain historical works also deserve mention:—

Ch'ien Han Shu, ch. 30.

Sui Shu, ch. 32-35.

Chiu T'ang Shu, ch. 46, 47.

Hsin T'ang Shu, ch. 57,60.

Sung Shih, ch. 202-209.

T'ung Chih (circa 1150), ch. 68.

To these of course must be added the great Catalogue of the Imperial Library:—

Ssu K'u Ch'uan Shu Tsung Mu T'i Yao (1790), ch. 99, 100.

CHAPTER 1

Laying Plans

[Ts'ao Kung, in defining the meaning of the Chinese for the title of this chapter, says it refers to the deliberations in the temple selected by the general for his temporary use, or as we should say, in his tent. See § 26.]

1. Sun Tzŭ said: The art of war is of vital importance to the State.

2. It is a matter of life and death, a road either to safety or to ruin. Hence it is a subject of inquiry which can on no account be neglected.

3. The art of war, then, is governed by five constant factors, to be taken into account in one's deliberations, when seeking to determine the conditions obtaining in the field.

4. These are: (1) The Moral Law; (2) Heaven; (3) Earth; (4) The Commander; (5) Method and discipline.

[It appears from what follows that Sun Tzŭ means by "Moral Law" a principle of harmony, not unlike the Tao of Lao Tzŭ in its moral aspect. One might be tempted to render it by "morale," were it not considered as an attribute of the *ruler* in § 13.]

5, 6. *The Moral Law* causes the people to be in complete accord with their ruler, so that they will follow him regardless of their lives, undismayed by any danger.

[Tu Yu quotes Wang Tzŭ as saying: "Without constant practice, the officers will be nervous and undecided when mustering for battle; without constant practice, the general will be wavering and irresolute when the crisis is at hand."]

7. *Heaven* signifies night and day, cold and heat, times and seasons.

[The commentators, I think, make an unnecessary mystery of two words here. Meng Shih refers to "the hard and the soft, waxing and waning" of Heaven. Wang Hsi, however, may be right in saying that what is meant is "the general economy of Heaven," including the five elements, the four seasons, wind and clouds, and other phenomena.]

8. *Earth* comprises distances, great and small; danger and security; open ground and narrow passes; the chances of life and death.

9. *The Commander* stands for the virtues of wisdom, sincerity, benevolence, courage and strictness.

[The five cardinal virtues of the Chinese are (1) humanity or benevolence; (2) uprightness of mind; (3) self-respect, self-control, or "proper feeling;" (4) wisdom; (5) sincerity or good faith. Here "wisdom" and "sincerity" are put before "humanity or benevolence," and the two military virtues of "courage" and "strictness" substituted for "uprightness of mind" and "self-respect, self-control, or 'proper feeling.'"]

10. By *Method and discipline* are to be understood the marshalling of the army in its proper subdivisions, the gradations of rank among the officers, the maintenance of roads by which supplies may reach the army, and the control of military expenditure.

11. These five heads should be familiar to every general: he who knows them will be victorious; he who knows them not will fail.

12. Therefore, in your deliberations, when seeking to determine the military conditions, let them be made the basis of a comparison, in this wise:—

13. (1) Which of the two sovereigns is imbued with the Moral law?

[I.e., "is in harmony with his subjects." Cf. § 5.]

(2) Which of the two generals has most ability?
(3) With whom lie the advantages derived from Heaven and Earth?

[See §§ 7, 8]

(4) On which side is discipline most rigorously enforced?

[Tu Mu alludes to the remarkable story of Ts'ao Ts'ao (A.D. 155-220), who was such a strict disciplinarian that once, in accordance with his own severe regulations against injury to standing crops, he condemned himself to death for having allowed his horse to shy into a field of corn! However, in lieu of losing his head, he was persuaded to satisfy his sense of justice by cutting off his hair. Ts'ao Ts'ao's own comment on the present passage is characteristically curt: "when you lay down a law, see that it is not disobeyed; if it is disobeyed the offender must be put to death."]

(5) Which army is the stronger?

[Morally as well as physically. As Mei Yao-ch'en puts it, freely rendered, "*esprit de corps* and 'big battalions.'"]

(6) On which side are officers and men more highly trained?

[Tu Yu quotes Wang Tzŭ as saying: "Without constant practice, the officers will be nervous and undecided when mustering for battle; without constant practice, the general will be wavering and irresolute when the crisis is at hand."]

(7) In which army is there the greater constancy both in reward and punishment?

[On which side is there the most absolute certainty that merit will be properly rewarded and misdeeds summarily punished?]

14. By means of these seven considerations I can forecast victory or defeat.

15. The general that hearkens to my counsel and acts upon it, will conquer:—let such a one be retained in command! The general that hearkens not to my counsel nor acts upon it, will suffer defeat:—let such a one be dismissed!

> [The form of this paragraph reminds us that Sun Tzŭ's treatise was composed expressly for the benefit of his patron Ho Lu, king of the Wu State.]

16. While heeding the profit of my counsel, avail yourself also of any helpful circumstances over and beyond the ordinary rules.

17. According as circumstances are favourable, one should modify one's plans.

> [Sun Tzŭ, as a practical soldier, will have none of the "bookish theoric." He cautions us here not to pin our faith to abstract principles; "for," as Chang Yu puts it, "while the main laws of strategy can be stated clearly enough for the benefit of all and sundry, you must be guided by the actions of the enemy in attempting to secure a favourable position in actual warfare." On the eve of the battle of Waterloo, Lord Uxbridge, commanding the cavalry, went to the Duke of Wellington in order to learn what his plans and calculations were for the morrow, because, as he explained, he might suddenly find himself Commander-in-chief and would be unable to frame new plans in a critical moment. The Duke listened quietly and then said: "Who will attack the first tomorrow—I or Bonaparte?" "Bonaparte," replied Lord Uxbridge. "Well," continued the Duke, "Bonaparte has not given me any idea of his projects; and as my plans will depend upon his, how can you expect me to tell you what mine are?"[1]]

---

1. "Words on Wellington," by Sir. W. Fraser.

18. All warfare is based on deception.

[The truth of this pithy and profound saying will be admitted by every soldier. Col. Henderson tells us that Wellington, great in so many military qualities, was especially distinguished by "the extraordinary skill with which he concealed his movements and deceived both friend and foe."]

19. Hence, when able to attack, we must seem unable; when using our forces, we must seem inactive; when we are near, we must make the enemy believe we are far away; when far away, we must make him believe we are near.

20. Hold out baits to entice the enemy. Feign disorder, and crush him.

[All commentators, except Chang Yu, say, "When he is in disorder, crush him." It is more natural to suppose that Sun Tzŭ is still illustrating the uses of deception in war.]

21. If he is secure at all points, be prepared for him. If he is in superior strength, evade him.

22. If your opponent is of choleric temper, seek to irritate him. Pretend to be weak, that he may grow arrogant.

[Wang Tzŭ, quoted by Tu Yu, says that the good tactician plays with his adversary as a cat plays with a mouse, first feigning weakness and immobility, and then suddenly pouncing upon him.]

23. If he is taking his ease, give him no rest.

[This is probably the meaning though Mei Yao-ch'en has the note: "while we are taking our ease, wait for the enemy to tire himself out." The *Yu Lan* has "Lure him on and tire him out."]

If his forces are united, separate them.

[Less plausible is the interpretation favoured by most of the commentators: "If sovereign and subject are in accord, put division between them."]

24. Attack him where he is unprepared, appear where you are not expected.

25. These military devices, leading to victory, must not be divulged beforehand.

26. Now the general who wins a battle makes many calculations in his temple ere the battle is fought.

> [Chang Yu tells us that in ancient times it was customary for a temple to be set apart for the use of a general who was about to take the field, in order that he might there elaborate his plan of campaign.]

The general who loses a battle makes but few calculations beforehand. Thus do many calculations lead to victory, and few calculations to defeat: how much more no calculation at all! It is by attention to this point that I can foresee who is likely to win or lose.

CHAPTER 2

Waging War

[Ts'ao Kung has the note: "He who wishes to fight must first count the cost," which prepares us for the discovery that the subject of the chapter is not what we might expect from the title, but is primarily a consideration of ways and means.]

1. Sun Tzŭ said: In the operations of war, where there are in the field a thousand swift chariots, as many heavy chariots, and a hundred thousand mail-clad soldiers,

[The "swift chariots" were lightly built and, according to Chang Yu, used for the attack; the "heavy chariots" were heavier, and designed for purposes of defence. Li Ch'uan, it is true, says that the latter were light, but this seems hardly probable. It is interesting to note the analogies between early Chinese warfare and that of the Homeric Greeks. In each case, the war-chariot was the important factor, forming as it did the nucleus round which was grouped a certain number of foot-soldiers. With regard to the numbers given here, we are informed that each swift chariot was accompanied by 75 footmen, and each heavy chariot by 25 footmen, so that the whole army would be divided up into a thousand battalions, each consisting of two chariots and a hundred men.]

with provisions enough to carry them a thousand *li*,

[2.78 modern *li* go to a mile. The length may have varied slightly since Sun Tzŭ's time.]

the expenditure at home and at the front, including entertainment of guests, small items such as glue and paint, and sums spent on chariots and armour, will reach the total of a thousand ounces of silver per day. Such is the cost of raising an army of 100,000 men.

2. When you engage in actual fighting, if victory is long in coming, the men's weapons will grow dull and their ardour will be damped. If you lay siege to a town, you will exhaust your strength.

3. Again, if the campaign is protracted, the resources of the State will not be equal to the strain.

4. Now, when your weapons are dulled, your ardour damped, your strength exhausted and your treasure spent, other chieftains will spring up to take advantage of your extremity. Then no man, however wise, will be able to avert the consequences that must ensue.

5. Thus, though we have heard of stupid haste in war, cleverness has never been seen associated with long delays.

[This concise and difficult sentence is not well explained by any of the commentators. Ts'ao Kung, Li Ch'uan, Meng Shih, Tu Yu, Tu Mu and Mei Yao-ch'en have notes to the effect that a general, though naturally stupid, may nevertheless conquer through sheer force of rapidity. Ho Shih says: "Haste may be stupid, but at any rate it saves expenditure of energy and treasure; protracted operations may be very clever, but they bring calamity in their train." Wang Hsi evades the difficulty by remarking: "Lengthy operations mean an army growing old, wealth being expended, an empty exchequer and distress among the people; true cleverness insures against the occurrence of such calamities." Chang Yu says: "So long as victory can be attained, stupid haste is preferable to clever dilatoriness." Now Sun Tzŭ says nothing whatever, except possibly by implication, about ill-considered haste being better than ingenious but lengthy operations. What he does say is something much more guarded, namely that, while speed may sometimes be injudicious, tardiness can never be anything but foolish—if only because it means impoverishment to the nation. In considering the point raised here by Sun Tzŭ, the classic example of Fabius Cunctator will inevitably occur to the mind. That general deliberately measured the endurance of Rome against that of Hannibals's isolated army, because it seemed to him that the latter was more likely to suffer from a long campaign in a strange country. But it is quite a moot question whether his tactics would have proved successful in the long run. Their reversal it is true, led to Cannae; but this only establishes a negative presumption in their favour.]

6. There is no instance of a country having benefited from prolonged warfare.

7. It is only one who is thoroughly acquainted with the evils of war that can thoroughly understand the profitable way of carrying it on.

[That is, with rapidity. Only one who knows the disastrous effects of a long war can realize the supreme importance of rapidity in bringing it to a close. Only two commentators seem to favour this interpretation, but it fits well into the logic of the context, whereas the rendering, "He who does not know the evils of war cannot appreciate its benefits," is distinctly pointless.]

8. The skilful soldier does not raise a second levy, neither are his supply-waggons loaded more than twice.

[Once war is declared, he will not waste precious time in waiting for reinforcements, nor will he return his army back for fresh supplies, but crosses the enemy's frontier without delay. This may seem an audacious policy to recommend, but with all great strategists, from Julius Caesar to Napoleon Bonaparte, the value of time—that is, being a little ahead of your opponent—has counted for more than either numerical superiority or the nicest calculations with regard to commissariat.]

9. Bring war material with you from home, but forage on the enemy. Thus the army will have food enough for its needs.

> [The Chinese word translated here as "war material" literally means "things to be used", and is meant in the widest sense. It includes all the impedimenta of an army, apart from provisions.]

10. Poverty of the State exchequer causes an army to be maintained by contributions from a distance. Contributing to maintain an army at a distance causes the people to be impoverished.

> [The beginning of this sentence does not balance properly with the next, though obviously intended to do so. The arrangement, moreover, is so awkward that I cannot help suspecting some corruption in the text. It never seems to occur to Chinese commentators that an emendation may be necessary for the sense, and we get no help from them there. The Chinese words Sun Tzŭ used to indicate the cause of the people's impoverishment clearly have reference to some system by which the husbandmen sent their contributions of corn to the army direct. But why should it fall on them to maintain an army in this way, except because the State or Government is too poor to do so?]

11. On the other hand, the proximity of an army causes prices to go up; and high prices cause the people's substance to be drained away.

> [Wang Hsi says high prices occur before the army has left its own territory. Ts'ao Kung understands it of an army that has already crossed the frontier.]

12. When their substance is drained away, the peasantry will be afflicted by heavy exactions.

13, 14. With this loss of substance and exhaustion of strength, the homes of the people will be stripped bare, and three-tenths of their incomes will be dissipated;

> [Tu Mu and Wang Hsi agree that the people are not mulcted not

of 3/10, but of 7/10, of their income. But this is hardly to be extracted from our text. Ho Shih has a characteristic tag: "The *people* being regarded as the essential part of the State, and *food* as the people's heaven, is it not right that those in authority should value and be careful of both?"]

while Government expenses for broken chariots, worn-out horses, breast-plates and helmets, bows and arrows, spears and shields, protective mantlets, draught-oxen and heavy waggons, will amount to four-tenths of its total revenue.

15. Hence a wise general makes a point of foraging on the enemy. One cartload of the enemy's provisions is equivalent to twenty of one's own, and likewise a single *picul* of his provender is equivalent to twenty from one's own store.

[Because twenty cartloads will be consumed in the process of transporting one cartload to the front. A *picul* is a unit of measure equal to 133.3 pounds (65.5 kilograms).]

16. Now in order to kill the enemy, our men must be roused to anger; that there may be advantage from defeating the enemy, they must have their rewards.

[Tu Mu says: "Rewards are necessary in order to make the soldiers see the advantage of beating the enemy; thus, when you capture spoils from the enemy, they must be used as rewards, so that all your men may have a keen desire to fight, each on his own account."]

17. Therefore in chariot fighting, when ten or more chariots have been taken, those should be rewarded who took the first. Our own flags should be substituted for those of the enemy, and the chariots mingled and used in conjunction with ours. The captured soldiers should be kindly treated and kept.

18. This is called, using the conquered foe to augment one's own strength.

19. In war, then, let your great object be victory, not lengthy campaigns.

> [As Ho Shih remarks: "War is not a thing to be trifled with." Sun Tzŭ here reiterates the main lesson which this chapter is intended to enforce."]

20. Thus it may be known that the leader of armies is the arbiter of the people's fate, the man on whom it depends whether the nation shall be in peace or in peril.

CHAPTER 3

Attack by Stratagem

1. Sun Tzŭ said: In the practical art of war, the best thing of all is to take the enemy's country whole and intact; to shatter and destroy it is not so good. So, too, it is better to capture an army entire than to destroy it, to capture a regiment, a detachment or a company entire than to destroy them.

[The equivalent to an army corps, according to Ssu-ma Fa, consisted nominally of 12500 men; according to Ts'ao Kung, the equivalent of a regiment contained 500 men, the equivalent to a detachment consists from any number between 100 and 500, and the equivalent of a company contains from 5 to 100 men. For the last two, however, Chang Yu gives the exact figures of 100 and 5 respectively.]

2. Hence to fight and conquer in all your battles is not supreme excellence; supreme excellence consists in breaking the enemy's resistance without fighting.

[Here again, no modern strategist but will approve the words of the old Chinese general. Moltke's greatest triumph, the capitulation of the huge French army at Sedan, was won practically without bloodshed.]

3. Thus the highest form of generalship is to baulk the enemy's plans;

[Perhaps the word "balk" falls short of expressing the full force of the Chinese word, which implies not an attitude of defence, whereby one might be content to foil the enemy's stratagems one after another, but an active policy of counter-attack. Ho Shih puts this very clearly in his note: "When the enemy has made a plan of attack against us, we must anticipate him by delivering our own attack first."]

the next best is to prevent the junction of the enemy's forces;

[Isolating him from his allies. We must not forget that Sun Tzŭ, in speaking of hostilities, always has in mind the numerous states or principalities into which the China of his day was split up.]

the next in order is to attack the enemy's army in the field;

[When he is already at full strength.]

and the worst policy of all is to besiege walled cities.

4. The rule is, not to besiege walled cities if it can possibly be avoided.

[Another sound piece of military theory. Had the Boers acted upon it in 1899, and refrained from dissipating their strength before Kimberley, Mafeking, or even Ladysmith, it is more than probable that they would have been masters of the situation before the British were ready seriously to oppose them.]

The preparation of mantlets, movable shelters, and various implements of war, will take up three whole months;

[It is not quite clear what the Chinese word, here translated as "mantlets", described. Ts'ao Kung simply defines them as "large shields," but we get a better idea of them from Li Ch'uan, who says they were to protect the heads of those who were assaulting the city walls at close quarters. This seems to suggest a sort of Roman *testudo*, ready made. Tu Mu says they were wheeled vehicles used in repelling attacks, but this is denied by Ch'en Hao. See *supra* II. 14. The name is also applied to turrets on city walls. Of the "movable shelters" we get a fairly clear description from several commentators. They were wooden missile-proof structures on four wheels, propelled from within, covered over with raw hides, and used in sieges to convey parties of men to and from the walls, for the purpose of filling up the encircling moat with earth. Tu Mu adds that they are now called "wooden donkeys."]

and the piling up of mounds over against the walls will take three months more.

[These were great mounds or ramparts of earth heaped up to the level of the enemy's walls in order to discover the weak points in the defence, and also to destroy the fortified turrets mentioned in the preceding note.]

5. The general, unable to control his irritation, will launch his men to the assault like swarming ants,

[This vivid simile of Ts'ao Kung is taken from the spectacle of an army of ants climbing a wall. The meaning is that the general, losing patience at the long delay, may make a premature attempt to storm the place before his engines of war are ready.]

with the result that one-third of his men are slain, while the town still remains untaken. Such are the disastrous effects of a siege.

[We are reminded of the terrible losses of the Japanese before Port Arthur, in the most recent siege which history has to record.]

6. Therefore the skilful leader subdues the enemy's troops without any fighting; he captures their cities without laying siege to them; he overthrows their kingdom without lengthy operations in the field.

[Chia Lin notes that he only overthrows the Government, but does no harm to individuals. The classical instance is Wu Wang, who after having put an end to the Yin dynasty was acclaimed "Father and mother of the people."]

7. With his forces intact he will dispute the mastery of the Empire, and thus, without losing a man, his triumph will be complete.

[Owing to the double meanings in the Chinese text, the latter part of the sentence is susceptible of quite a different meaning: "And thus, the weapon not being blunted by use, its keenness remains perfect."]

This is the method of attacking by stratagem.

8. It is the rule in war, if our forces are ten to the enemy's one, to surround him; if five to one, to attack him;

[Straightway, without waiting for any further advantage.]

if twice as numerous, to divide our army into two.

[Tu Mu takes exception to the saying; and at first sight, indeed, it appears to violate a fundamental principle of war. Ts'ao Kung, however, gives a clue to Sun Tzŭ's meaning: "Being two to the enemy's one, we may use one part of our army in the regular way, and the other for some special diversion." Chang Yu thus further elucidates the point: "If our force is twice as numerous as that of the enemy, it should be split up into two divisions, one to meet the enemy in front, and one to fall upon his rear; if he replies to the frontal attack, he may be crushed from behind; if to the rearward attack, he may be crushed in front." This is what is meant by saying that 'one part may be used in the regular way, and the other for some special diversion.' Tu Mu does not understand that dividing one's army is simply an irregular, just as concentrating it is the regular, strategical method, and he is too hasty in calling this a mistake."]

9. If equally matched, we can offer battle;

[Li Ch'uan, followed by Ho Shih, gives the following paraphrase: "If attackers and attacked are equally matched in strength, only the able general will fight."]

if slightly inferior in numbers, we can avoid the enemy;

[The meaning, "we can *watch* the enemy," is certainly a great improvement on the above; but unfortunately there appears to be no very good authority for the variant. Chang Yu reminds us that the saying only applies if the other factors are equal; a small difference in numbers is often more than counterbalanced by superior energy and discipline.]

if quite unequal in every way, we can flee from him.

10. Hence, though an obstinate fight may be made by a small force, in the end it must be captured by the larger force.

11. Now the general is the bulwark of the State: if the bulwark is complete at all points; the State will be strong; if the bulwark is defective, the State will be weak.

[As Li Ch'uan tersely puts it: "Gap indicates deficiency; if the general's ability is not perfect (i.e. if he is not thoroughly versed in his profession), his army will lack strength."]

12. There are three ways in which a ruler can bring misfortune upon his army:—

13. (1) By commanding the army to advance or to retreat, being ignorant of the fact that it cannot obey. This is called hobbling the army.

[Li Ch'uan adds the comment: "It is like tying together the legs of a thoroughbred, so that it is unable to gallop." One would naturally think of "the ruler" in this passage as being at home, and trying to direct the movements of his army from a distance.

But the commentators understand just the reverse, and quote the saying of T'ai Kung: "A kingdom should not be governed from without, and army should not be directed from within." Of course it is true that, during an engagement, or when in close touch with the enemy, the general should not be in the thick of his own troops, but a little distance apart. Otherwise, he will be liable to misjudge the position as a whole, and give wrong orders.]

14. (2) By attempting to govern an army in the same way as he administers a kingdom, being ignorant of the conditions which obtain in an army. This causes restlessness in the soldier's minds.

[Ts'ao Kung's note is, freely translated: "The military sphere and the civil sphere are wholly distinct; you can't handle an army in kid gloves." And Chang Yu says: "Humanity and justice are the principles on which to govern a state, but not an army; opportunism and flexibility, on the other hand, are military rather than civil virtues to assimilate the governing of an army"—to that of a State, understood.]

15. (3) By employing the officers of his army without discrimination,

[That is, he is not careful to use the right man in the right place.]

through ignorance of the military principle of adaptation to circumstances. This shakes the confidence of the soldiers.

[I follow Mei Yao-ch'en here. The other commentators refer not to the ruler, as in §§ 13, 14, but to the officers he employs. Thus Tu Yu says: "If a general is ignorant of the principle of adaptability, he must not be entrusted with a position of authority." Tu Mu quotes: "The skilful employer of men will employ the wise man, the brave man, the covetous man, and the stupid man. For the wise man delights in establishing his merit, the brave man likes to show his courage in action, the covetous man is quick at seizing advantages, and the stupid man has no fear of death."]

16. But when the army is restless and distrustful, trouble is sure to come from the other feudal princes. This is simply bringing anarchy into the army, and flinging victory away.

17. Thus we may know that there are five essentials for victory:

(1) He will win who knows when to fight and when not to fight.

[Chang Yu says: If he can fight, he advances and takes the offensive; if he cannot fight, he retreats and remains on the defensive. He will invariably conquer who knows whether it is right to take the offensive or the defensive.]

(2) He will win who knows how to handle both superior and inferior forces.

[This is not merely the general's ability to estimate numbers correctly, as Li Ch'uan and others make out. Chang Yu expounds the saying more satisfactorily: "By applying the art of war, it is possible with a lesser force to defeat a greater, and *vice versa.* The secret lies in an eye for locality, and in not letting the right moment slip. Thus Wu Tzŭ says: 'With a superior force, make for easy ground; with an inferior one, make for difficult ground.'"]

(3) He will win whose army is animated by the same spirit throughout all its ranks.
(4) He will win who, prepared himself, waits to take the enemy unprepared.
(5) He will win who has military capacity and is not interfered with by the sovereign.

[Tu Yu quotes Wang Tzŭ as saying: "It is the sovereign's function to give broad instructions, but to decide on battle it is the function of the general." It is needless to dilate on the military disasters which have been caused by undue interference with operations in the field on the part of the home government. Napoleon

[undoubtedly owed much of his extraordinary success to the fact that he was not hampered by central authority.]

Victory lies in the knowledge of these five points.

[Literally, "These five things are knowledge of the principle of victory."]

18. Hence the saying: If you know the enemy and know yourself, you need not fear the result of a hundred battles. If you know yourself but not the enemy, for every victory gained you will also suffer a defeat.

[Li Ch'uan cites the case of Fu Chien, prince of Ch'in, who in 383 A.D. marched with a vast army against the Chin Emperor. When warned not to despise an enemy who could command the services of such men as Hsieh An and Huan Ch'ung, he boastfully replied: "I have the population of eight provinces at my back, infantry and horsemen to the number of one million; why, they could dam up the Yangtsze River itself by merely throwing their whips into the stream. What danger have I to fear?" Nevertheless, his forces were soon after disastrously routed at the Fei River, and he was obliged to beat a hasty retreat.]

If you know neither the enemy nor yourself, you will succumb in every battle.

[Chang Yu said: "Knowing the enemy enables you to take the offensive, knowing yourself enables you to stand on the defensive." He adds: "Attack is the secret of defence; defence is the planning of an attack." It would be hard to find a better epitome of the root-principle of war.]

CHAPTER 4

Tactical Dispositions

[Ts'ao Kung explains the Chinese meaning of the words for the title of this chapter: "marching and countermarching on the part of the two armies with a view to discovering each other's condition." Tu Mu says: "It is through the dispositions of an army that its condition may be discovered. Conceal your dispositions, and your condition will remain secret, which leads to victory; show your dispositions, and your condition will become patent, which leads to defeat." Wang Hsi remarks that the good general can "secure success by modifying his tactics to meet those of the enemy."]

1. Sun Tzŭ said: The good fighters of old first put themselves beyond the possibility of defeat, and then waited for an opportunity of defeating the enemy.

2. To secure ourselves against defeat lies in our own hands, but the opportunity of defeating the enemy is provided by the enemy himself.

[That is, of course, by a mistake on the enemy's part.]

3. Thus the good fighter is able to secure himself against defeat,

[Chang Yu says this is done, "By concealing the disposition

of his troops, covering up his tracks, and taking unremitting precautions."]

but cannot make certain of defeating the enemy.

4. Hence the saying: One may *know* how to conquer without being able to *do* it.

5. Security against defeat implies defensive tactics; ability to defeat the enemy means taking the offensive.

[I retain the sense found in a similar passage in §§ 1-3, in spite of the fact that the commentators are all against me. The meaning they give, "He who cannot conquer takes the defensive," is plausible enough.]

6. Standing on the defensive indicates insufficient strength; attacking, a superabundance of strength.

7. The general who is skilled in defence hides in the most secret recesses of the earth;

[Literally, "hides under the ninth earth," which is a metaphor indicating the utmost secrecy and concealment, so that the enemy may not know his whereabouts.]

he who is skilled in attack flashes forth from the topmost heights of heaven.

[Another metaphor, implying that he falls on his adversary like a thunderbolt, against which there is no time to prepare. This is the opinion of most of the commentators.]

Thus on the one hand we have ability to protect ourselves; on the other, a victory that is complete.

8. To see victory only when it is within the ken of the common herd is not the acme of excellence.

[As Ts'ao Kung remarks, "the thing is to see the plant before it has germinated," to foresee the event before the action has begun. Li Ch'uan alludes to the story of Han Hsin who, when about to attack the vastly superior army of Chao, which was strongly entrenched in the city of Ch'eng-an, said to his officers: "Gentlemen, we are going to annihilate the enemy, and shall meet again at dinner." The officers hardly took his words seriously, and gave a very dubious assent. But Han Hsin had already worked out in his mind the details of a clever stratagem, whereby, as he foresaw, he was able to capture the city and inflict a crushing defeat on his adversary.]

9. Neither is it the acme of excellence if you fight and conquer and the whole Empire says, "Well done!"

[True excellence being, as Tu Mu says: "To plan secretly, to move surreptitiously, to foil the enemy's intentions and balk his schemes, so that at last the day may be won without shedding a drop of blood." Sun Tzŭ reserves his approbation for things that

"the world's coarse thumb
And finger fail to plumb."]

10. To lift an autumn hair is no sign of great strength;

["Autumn hair" is explained as the fur of a hare, which is finest in autumn, when it begins to grow afresh. The phrase is a very common one in Chinese writers.]

to see sun and moon is no sign of sharp sight; to hear the noise of thunder is no sign of a quick ear.

[Ho Shih gives as real instances of strength, sharp sight and quick hearing: Wu Huo, who could lift a tripod weighing 250 stone; Li Chu, who at a distance of a hundred paces could see objects no bigger than a mustard seed; and Shih K'uang, a blind musician who could hear the footsteps of a mosquito.]

11. What the ancients called a clever fighter is one who not only wins, but excels in winning with ease.

[The last half is literally "one who, conquering, excels in easy conquering." Mei Yao-ch'en says: "He who only sees the obvious, wins his battles with difficulty; he who looks below the surface of things, wins with ease."]

12. Hence his victories bring him neither reputation for wisdom nor credit for courage.

[Tu Mu explains this very well: "Inasmuch as his victories are gained over circumstances that have not come to light, the world as large knows nothing of them, and he wins no reputation for wisdom; inasmuch as the hostile state submits before there has been any bloodshed, he receives no credit for courage."]

13. He wins his battles by making no mistakes.

[Ch'en Hao says: "He plans no superfluous marches, he devises no futile attacks." The connection of ideas is thus explained by Chang Yu: "One who seeks to conquer by sheer strength, clever though he may be at winning pitched battles, is also liable on occasion to be vanquished; whereas he who can look into the future and discern conditions that are not yet manifest, will never make a blunder and therefore invariably win."]

Making no mistakes is what establishes the certainty of victory, for it means conquering an enemy that is already defeated.

14. Hence the skilful fighter puts himself into a position which makes defeat impossible, and does not miss the moment for defeating the enemy.

[A "counsel of perfection" as Tu Mu truly observes. "Position" need not be confined to the actual ground occupied by the troops. It includes all the arrangements and preparations which a wise general will make to increase the safety of his army.]

15. Thus it is that in war the victorious strategist only seeks battle after the victory has been won, whereas he who is destined to defeat first fights and afterwards looks for victory.

[Ho Shih thus expounds the paradox: "In warfare, first lay plans which will ensure victory, and then lead your army to battle; if you will not begin with stratagem but rely on brute strength alone, victory will no longer be assured."]

16. The consummate leader cultivates the moral law, and strictly adheres to method and discipline; thus it is in his power to control success.

17. In respect of military method, we have, firstly, Measurement; secondly, Estimation of quantity; thirdly, Calculation; fourthly, Balancing of chances; fifthly, Victory.

18. Measurement owes its existence to Earth; Estimation of quantity to Measurement; Calculation to Estimation of quantity; Balancing of chances to Calculation; and Victory to Balancing of chances.

[It is not easy to distinguish the four terms very clearly in the Chinese. The first seems to be surveying and measurement of the ground, which enable us to form an estimate of the enemy's strength, and to make calculations based on the data thus obtained; we are thus led to a general weighing-up, or comparison of the enemy's chances with our own; if the latter turn the scale, then victory ensues. The chief difficulty lies in third term, which in the Chinese some commentators take as a calculation of *numbers*, thereby making it nearly synonymous with the second term. Perhaps the second term should be thought of as a consideration of the enemy's general position or condition, while the third term is the estimate of his numerical strength. On the other hand, Tu Mu says: "The question of relative strength having been settled, we can bring the varied resources of cunning into play." Ho Shih seconds this interpretation, but weakens it. However, it points to the third term as being a calculation of numbers.]

19. A victorious army opposed to a routed one, is as a pound's weight placed in the scale against a single grain.

[Literally, "a victorious army is like an *i* (20 oz.) weighed against a *shu* (1/24 oz.); a routed army is a *shu* weighed against an *i*." The point is simply the enormous advantage which a disciplined force, flushed with victory, has over one demoralized by defeat. Legge, in his note on Mencius, I. 2. ix. 2, makes the *i* to be 24 Chinese ounces, and corrects Chu Hsi's statement that it equaled 20 oz. only. But Li Ch'uan of the T'ang dynasty here gives the same figure as Chu Hsi.]

20. The onrush of a conquering force is like the bursting of pent-up waters into a chasm a thousand fathoms deep. So much for tactical dispositions.

CHAPTER 5

Energy

1. Sun Tzŭ said: The control of a large force is the same principle as the control of a few men: it is merely a question of dividing up their numbers.

[That is, cutting up the army into regiments, companies, etc., with subordinate officers in command of each. Tu Mu reminds us of Han Hsin's famous reply to the first Han Emperor, who once said to him: "How large an army do you think I could lead?" "Not more than 100,000 men, your Majesty." "And you?" asked the Emperor. "Oh!" he answered, "the more the better."]

2. Fighting with a large army under your command is nowise different from fighting with a small one: it is merely a question of instituting signs and signals.

3. To ensure that your whole host may withstand the brunt of the enemy's attack and remain unshaken—this is effected by manœuvers direct and indirect.

[We now come to one of the most interesting parts of Sun Tzŭ's treatise, the discussion of the *cheng* and the *ch'i*. As it is by no means easy to grasp the full significance of these two terms, or to render them consistently by good English equivalents; it may be as well to tabulate some of the commentators' remarks on the subject before proceeding further. Li Ch'uan: "Facing the enemy is *cheng*, making lateral diversion is *ch'i*." Chia Lin: "In presence of the enemy, your troops should be arrayed in normal fashion, but in order to secure victory abnormal manœuvers must be employed." Mei Yao-ch'en: "*Ch'i* is active, *cheng* is passive; passivity means waiting for an opportunity, activity brings the victory itself." Ho Shih: "We must cause the enemy to regard our straightforward attack as one that is secretly designed, and vice versa; thus *cheng* may also be *ch'i*, and *ch'i* may also be *cheng*." He instances the famous exploit of Han Hsin, who when marching ostensibly against Lin-chin (now Chao-i in Shensi), suddenly threw a large force across the Yellow River in wooden tubs, utterly disconcerting his opponent. [Ch'ien Han Shu, ch. 3.] Here, we are told, the march on Lin-chin was *cheng*, and the surprise manoeuver was *ch'i*. Chang Yu gives the following summary of opinions on the words: "Military writers do not agree with regard to the meaning of *ch'i* and *cheng*. Wei Liao Tzŭ [4th cent. B.C.] says: 'Direct warfare favours frontal attacks, indirect warfare attacks from the rear.' Ts'ao Kung says: 'Going straight out to join battle is a direct operation; appearing on the enemy's rear is an indirect manoeuver.' Li Wei-kung [6th and 7th cent. A.D.] says: 'In war, to march straight ahead is *cheng*; turning movements, on the other hand, are *ch'i*.' These writers simply regard *cheng* as *cheng*, and *ch'i* as *ch'i*; they do not note that the two are mutually interchangeable and run into each other like the two sides of a circle [see infra, § 11]. A comment on the T'ang Emperor T'ai Tsung goes to the root of the matter: 'A *ch'i* manœuver may be *cheng*, if we make the enemy look upon it as *cheng*; then our real attack will be *ch'i*, and vice versa. The whole secret lies in confusing the enemy, so that he cannot fathom our real intent.'" To put it perhaps a little more clearly: any attack or other operation is *cheng*, on which the enemy has had his attention fixed; whereas that is *ch'i*, which takes him by surprise or comes from an unexpected quarter. If the enemy perceives a movement which is meant to be *ch'i*, it immediately becomes *cheng*.]

4. That the impact of your army may be like a grindstone dashed against an egg—this is effected by the science of weak points and strong.

5. In all fighting, the direct method may be used for joining battle, but indirect methods will be needed in order to secure victory.

[Chang Yu says: "Steadily develop indirect tactics, either by pounding the enemy's flanks or falling on his rear." A brilliant example of "indirect tactics" which decided the fortunes of a campaign was Lord Roberts' night march round the Peiwar Kotal in the second Afghan war.[1]]

6. Indirect tactics, efficiently applied, are inexhausible as Heaven and Earth, unending as the flow of rivers and streams; like the sun and moon, they end but to begin anew; like the four seasons, they pass away but to return once more.

[Tu Yu and Chang Yu understand this of the permutations of *ch'i* and *cheng*. But at present Sun Tzŭ is not speaking of *cheng* at all, unless, indeed, we suppose with Cheng Yu-hsien that a clause relating to it has fallen out of the text. Of course, as has already been pointed out, the two are so inextricably interwoven in all military operations, that they cannot really be considered apart. Here we simply have an expression, in figurative language, of the almost infinite resource of a great leader.]

7. There are not more than five musical notes, yet the combinations of these five give rise to more melodies than can ever be heard.

8. There are not more than five primary colours (blue, yellow, red, white, and black), yet in combination they produce more hues than can ever be seen.

---

1. "Forty-one Years in India," chapter 46.

9. There are not more than five cardinal tastes (sour, acrid, salt, sweet, bitter), yet combinations of them yield more flavours than can ever be tasted.

10. In battle, there are not more than two methods of attack—the direct and the indirect; yet these two in combination give rise to an endless series of manoeuvers.

11. The direct and the indirect lead on to each other in turn. It is like moving in a circle—you never come to an end. Who can exhaust the possibilities of their combination?

12. The onset of troops is like the rush of a torrent which will even roll stones along in its course.

13. The quality of decision is like the well-timed swoop of a falcon which enables it to strike and destroy its victim.

[The Chinese here is tricky and a certain key word in the context it is used defies the best efforts of the translator. Tu Mu defines this word as "the measurement or estimation of distance." But this meaning does not quite fit the illustrative simile in § 15. Applying this definition to the falcon, it seems to me to denote that instinct of *self-restraint* which keeps the bird from swooping on its quarry until the right moment, together with the power of judging when the right moment has arrived. The analogous quality in soldiers is the highly important one of being able to reserve their fire until the very instant at which it will be most effective. When the "Victory" went into action at Trafalgar at hardly more than drifting pace, she was for several minutes exposed to a storm of shot and shell before replying with a single gun. Nelson coolly waited until he was within close range, when the broadside he brought to bear worked fearful havoc on the enemy's nearest ships.]

14. Therefore the good fighter will be terrible in his onset, and prompt in his decision.

[The word "decision" would have reference to the measurement of distance mentioned above, letting the enemy get near before striking. But I cannot help thinking that Sun Tzŭ meant to use the word in a figurative sense comparable to our own idiom "short and sharp." Cf. Wang Hsi's note, which after describing the falcon's mode of attack, proceeds: "This is just how the 'psychological moment' should be seized in war."]

15. Energy may be likened to the bending of a crossbow; decision, to the releasing of the trigger.

[None of the commentators seem to grasp the real point of the simile of energy and the force stored up in the bent cross-bow until released by the finger on the trigger.]

16. Amid the turmoil and tumult of battle, there may be seeming disorder and yet no real disorder at all; amid confusion and chaos, your array may be without head or tail, yet it will be proof against defeat.

[Mei Yao-ch'en says: "The subdivisions of the army having been previously fixed, and the various signals agreed upon, the separating and joining, the dispersing and collecting which will take place in the course of a battle, may give the appearance of disorder when no real disorder is possible. Your formation may be without head or tail, your dispositions all topsy-turvy, and yet a rout of your forces quite out of the question."]

17. Simulated disorder postulates perfect discipline; simulated fear postulates courage; simulated weakness postulates strength.

[In order to make the translation intelligible, it is necessary to tone down the sharply paradoxical form of the original. Ts'ao Kung throws out a hint of the meaning in his brief note: "These things all serve to destroy formation and conceal one's condition." But Tu Mu is the first to put it quite plainly: "If you wish to feign confusion in order to lure the enemy on, you must first have perfect discipline; if you wish to display timidity in order to entrap the enemy, you must have extreme courage; if you wish to parade your weakness in order to make the enemy over-confident, you must have exceeding strength."]

18. Hiding order beneath the cloak of disorder is simply a question of subdivision;

[See *supra*, § 1.]

concealing courage under a show of timidity presupposes a fund of latent energy;

[The commentators strongly understand a certain Chinese word here differently than anywhere else in this chapter. Thus Tu Mu says: "seeing that we are favourably circumstanced and yet make no move, the enemy will believe that we are really afraid."]

masking strength with weakness is to be effected by tactical dispositions.

[Chang Yu relates the following anecdote of Kao Tsu, the first Han Emperor: "Wishing to crush the Hsiung-nu, he sent out spies to report on their condition. But the Hsiung-nu, forewarned, carefully concealed all their able-bodied men and well-fed horses, and only allowed infirm soldiers and emaciated cattle to be seen. The result was that spies one and all recommended the Emperor to deliver his attack. Lou Ching alone opposed them, saying: 'When two countries go to war, they are naturally inclined to make an ostentatious display of their strength. Yet our spies have seen nothing but old age and infirmity. This is surely some ruse on the part of the enemy, and it would be unwise for us to attack.' The Emperor, however, disregarding this advice, fell into the trap and found himself surrounded at Po-teng."]

19. Thus one who is skilful at keeping the enemy on the move maintains deceitful appearances, according to which the enemy will act.

[Ts'ao Kung's note is "Make a display of weakness and want." Tu Mu says: "If our force happens to be superior to the enemy's, weakness may be simulated in order to lure him on; but if inferior, he must be led to believe that we are strong, in order that he may keep off. In fact, all the enemy's movements should be determined by the signs that we choose to give him." Note the following anecdote of Sun Pin, a descendent of Sun Wu: In 341 B.C., the Ch'i State being at war with Wei, sent T'ien Chi and Sun Pin against the general P'ang Chuan, who happened to be a deadly personal enemy of the later. Sun Pin said: "The Ch'i State has a reputation for cowardice, and therefore our adversary despises us. Let us turn this circumstance to account." Accordingly, when the army had crossed the border into Wei territory, he gave orders to show 100,000 fires on the first night, 50,000 on the next, and the night after only 20,000. P'ang Chuan pursued them hotly, saying to himself: "I knew these men of Ch'i were cowards: their numbers have already fallen away by more than half." In his retreat, Sun Pin came to a narrow defile, which he calculated that his pursuers would reach after dark. Here he had a tree stripped of its bark, and inscribed upon it the words: "Under this tree shall P'ang Chuan die." Then, as night began to fall, he placed a strong body of archers in ambush near by, with orders to shoot directly if they saw a light. Later on, P'ang Chuan arrived at the spot, and noticing the tree, struck a light in order to read what was written on it. His body was immediately riddled by a volley of arrows, and his whole army thrown into confusion. [The above is Tu Mu's version of the story; the *Shih Chi*, less dramatically but probably with more historical truth, makes P'ang Chuan cut his own throat with an exclamation of despair, after the rout of his army.]]

He sacrifices something, that the enemy may snatch at it.

20. By holding out baits, he keeps him on the march; then with a body of picked men he lies in wait for him.

[With an emendation suggested by Li Ching, this then reads, "He lies in wait with the main body of his troops."]

21. The clever combatant looks to the effect of combined energy, and does not require too much from individuals.

[Tu Mu says: "He first of all considers the power of his army in the bulk; afterwards he takes individual talent into account, and uses each men according to his capabilities. He does not demand perfection from the untalented."]

Hence his ability to pick out the right men and utilise combined energy.

22. When he utilises combined energy, his fighting men become as it were like unto rolling logs or stones. For it is the nature of a log or stone to remain motionless on level ground, and to move when on a slope; if four-cornered, to come to a standstill, but if round-shaped, to go rolling down.

[Ts'au Kung calls this "the use of natural or inherent power."]

23. Thus the energy developed by good fighting men is as the momentum of a round stone rolled down a mountain thousands of feet in height. So much on the subject of energy.

[The chief lesson of this chapter, in Tu Mu's opinion, is the paramount importance in war of rapid evolutions and sudden rushes. "Great results," he adds, "can thus be achieved with small forces."]

CHAPTER 6

Weak Points and Strong

[Chang Yu attempts to explain the sequence of chapters as follows: "Chapter IV, on Tactical Dispositions, treated of the offensive and the defensive; chapter V, on Energy, dealt with direct and indirect methods. The good general acquaints himself first with the theory of attack and defence, and then turns his attention to direct and indirect methods. He studies the art of varying and combining these two methods before proceeding to the subject of weak and strong points. For the use of direct or indirect methods arises out of attack and defence, and the perception of weak and strong points depends again on the above methods. Hence the present chapter comes immediately after the chapter on Energy."]

1. Sun Tzŭ said: Whoever is first in the field and awaits the coming of the enemy, will be fresh for the fight; whoever is second in the field and has to hasten to battle, will arrive exhausted.

2. Therefore the clever combatant imposes his will on the enemy, but does not allow the enemy's will to be imposed on him.

[One mark of a great soldier is that he fight on his own terms or fights not at all.[1]]

---

1. See Col. Henderson's biography of Stonewall Jackson, 1902 ed., vol. II, p. 490.

3. By holding out advantages to him, he can cause the enemy to approach of his own accord; or, by inflicting damage, he can make it impossible for the enemy to draw near.

> [In the first case, he will entice him with a bait; in the second, he will strike at some important point which the enemy will have to defend.]

4. If the enemy is taking his ease, he can harass him;

> [This passage may be cited as evidence against Mei Yao-Ch'en's interpretation of I. § 23.]

if well supplied with food, he can starve him out; if quietly encamped, he can force him to move.

5. Appear at points which the enemy must hasten to defend; march swiftly to places where you are not expected.

6. An army may march great distances without distress, if it marches through country where the enemy is not.

> [Ts'ao Kung sums up very well: "Emerge from the void [q.d. like "a bolt from the blue"], strike at vulnerable points, shun places that are defended, attack in unexpected quarters."]

7. You can be sure of succeeding in your attacks if you only attack places which are undefended.

> [Wang Hsi explains "undefended places" as "weak points; that is to say, where the general is lacking in capacity, or the soldiers in spirit; where the walls are not strong enough, or the precautions not strict enough; where relief comes too late, or provisions are too scanty, or the defenders are variance amongst themselves."]

You can ensure the safety of your defence if you only hold positions that cannot be attacked.

> [*I.e.*, where there are none of the weak points mentioned above. There is rather a nice point involved in the interpretation of this

later clause. Tu Mu, Ch'en Hao, and Mei Yao-ch'en assume the meaning to be: "In order to make your defence quite safe, you must defend *even* those places that are not likely to be attacked;" and Tu Mu adds: "How much more, then, those that will be attacked." Taken thus, however, the clause balances less well with the preceding—always a consideration in the highly antithetical style which is natural to the Chinese. Chang Yu, therefore, seems to come nearer the mark in saying: "He who is skilled in attack flashes forth from the topmost heights of heaven [see IV. § 7], making it impossible for the enemy to guard against him. This being so, the places that I shall attack are precisely those that the enemy cannot defend.... He who is skilled in defence hides in the most secret recesses of the earth, making it impossible for the enemy to estimate his whereabouts. This being so, the places that I shall hold are precisely those that the enemy cannot attack."]

8. Hence that general is skilful in attack whose opponent does not know what to defend; and he is skilful in defence whose opponent does not know what to attack.

[An aphorism which puts the whole art of war in a nutshell.]

9. O divine art of subtlety and secrecy! Through you we learn to be invisible, through you inaudible;

[Literally, "without form or sound," but it is said of course with reference to the enemy.]

and hence we can hold the enemy's fate in our hands.

10. You may advance and be absolutely irresistible, if you make for the enemy's weak points; you may retire and be safe from pursuit if your movements are more rapid than those of the enemy.

11. If we wish to fight, the enemy can be forced to an engagement even though he be sheltered behind a high rampart and a deep ditch. All we need do is attack some other place that he will be obliged to relieve.

[Tu Mu says: "If the enemy is the invading party, we can cut his line of communications and occupy the roads by which he will have to return; if we are the invaders, we may direct our attack against the sovereign himself." It is clear that Sun Tzŭ, unlike certain generals in the late Boer war, was no believer in frontal attacks.]

12. If we do not wish to fight, we can prevent the enemy from engaging us even though the lines of our encampment be merely traced out on the ground. All we need do is to throw something odd and unaccountable in his way.

[This extremely concise expression is intelligibly paraphrased by Chia Lin: "even though we have constructed neither wall nor ditch." Li Ch'uan says: "we puzzle him by strange and unusual dispositions;" and Tu Mu finally clinches the meaning by three illustrative anecdotes—one of Chu-ko Liang, who when occupying Yang-p'ing and about to be attacked by Ssu-ma I, suddenly struck his colors, stopped the beating of the drums, and flung open the city gates, showing only a few men engaged in sweeping and sprinkling the ground. This unexpected proceeding had the intended effect; for Ssu-ma I, suspecting an ambush, actually drew off his army and retreated. What Sun Tzŭ is advocating here, therefore, is nothing more nor less than the timely use of "bluff."]

13. By discovering the enemy's dispositions and remaining invisible ourselves, we can keep our forces concentrated, while the enemy's must be divided.

[The conclusion is perhaps not very obvious, but Chang Yu (after Mei Yao-ch'en) rightly explains it thus: "If the enemy's dispositions are visible, we can make for him in one body; whereas, our own dispositions being kept secret, the enemy will be obliged to divide his forces in order to guard against attack from every quarter."]

14. We can form a single united body, while the enemy must split up into fractions. Hence there will be a whole pitted against

separate parts of a whole, which means that we shall be many to the enemy's few.

15. And if we are able thus to attack an inferior force with a superior one, our opponents will be in dire straits.

16. The spot where we intend to fight must not be made known; for then the enemy will have to prepare against a possible attack at several different points;

> [Sheridan once explained the reason of General Grant's victories by saying that "while his opponents were kept fully employed wondering what he was going to do, *he* was thinking most of what he was going to do himself."]

and his forces being thus distributed in many directions, the numbers we shall have to face at any given point will be proportionately few.

17. For should the enemy strengthen his van, he will weaken his rear; should he strengthen his rear, he will weaken his van; should he strengthen his left, he will weaken his right; should he strengthen his right, he will weaken his left. If he sends reinforcements everywhere, he will everywhere be weak.

> [In Frederick the Great's *Instructions to his Generals* we read: "A defensive war is apt to betray us into too frequent detachment. Those generals who have had but little experience attempt to protect every point, while those who are better acquainted with their profession, having only the capital object in view, guard against a decisive blow, and acquiesce in small misfortunes to avoid greater."]

18. Numerical weakness comes from having to prepare against possible attacks; numerical strength, from compelling our adversary to make these preparations against us.

> [The highest generalship, in Col. Henderson's words, is "to compel the enemy to disperse his army, and then to concentrate superior force against each fraction in turn."]

19. Knowing the place and the time of the coming battle, we may concentrate from the greatest distances in order to fight.

[What Sun Tzŭ evidently has in mind is that nice calculation of distances and that masterly employment of strategy which enable a general to divide his army for the purpose of a long and rapid march, and afterwards to effect a junction at precisely the right spot and the right hour in order to confront the enemy in overwhelming strength. Among many such successful junctions which military history records, one of the most dramatic and decisive was the appearance of Blucher just at the critical moment on the field of Waterloo.]

20. But if neither time nor place be known, then the left wing will be impotent to succour the right, the right equally impotent to succour the left, the van unable to relieve the rear, or the rear to support the van. How much more so if the furthest portions of the army are anything under a hundred *li* apart, and even the nearest are separated by several *li*!

[The Chinese of this last sentence is a little lacking in precision, but the mental picture we are required to draw is probably that of an army advancing towards a given rendezvous in separate columns, each of which has orders to be there on a fixed date. If the general allows the various detachments to proceed at haphazard, without precise instructions as to the time and place of meeting, the enemy will be able to annihilate the army in detail. Chang Yu's note may be worth quoting here: "If we do not know the place where our opponents mean to concentrate or the day on which they will join battle, our unity will be forfeited through our preparations for defence, and the positions we hold will be insecure. Suddenly happening upon a powerful foe, we shall be brought to battle in a flurried condition, and no mutual support will be possible between wings, vanguard or rear, especially if there is any great distance between the foremost and hindmost divisions of the army."]

21. Though according to my estimate the soldiers of Yüeh exceed our own in number, that shall advantage them nothing in the matter of victory. I say then that victory can be achieved.

[Alas for these brave words! The long feud between the two states ended in 473 B.C. with the total defeat of Wu by Kou Chien and its incorporation in Yüeh. This was doubtless long after Sun Tzŭ's death. With his present assertion compare IV. § 4. Chang Yu is the only one to point out the seeming discrepancy, which he thus goes on to explain: "In the chapter on Tactical Dispositions it is said, 'One may *know* how to conquer without being able to *do* it,' whereas here we have the statement that 'victory' can be achieved.' The explanation is, that in the former chapter, where the offensive and defensive are under discussion, it is said that if the enemy is fully prepared, one cannot make certain of beating him. But the present passage refers particularly to the soldiers of Yüeh who, according to Sun Tzŭ's calculations, will be kept in ignorance of the time and place of the impending struggle. That is why he says here that victory can be achieved."]

22. Though the enemy be stronger in numbers, we may prevent him from fighting. Scheme so as to discover his plans and the likelihood of their success.

[An alternative reading offered by Chia Lin is: "Know beforehand all plans conducive to our success and to the enemy's failure."]

23. Rouse him, and learn the principle of his activity or inactivity.

[Chang Yu tells us that by noting the joy or anger shown by the enemy on being thus disturbed, we shall be able to conclude whether his policy is to lie low or the reverse. He instances the action of Cho-ku Liang, who sent the scornful present of a woman's head-dress to Ssu-ma I, in order to goad him out of his Fabian tactics.]

Force him to reveal himself, so as to find out his vulnerable spots.

24. Carefully compare the opposing army with your own, so that you may know where strength is superabundant and where it is deficient.

[Cf. IV. § 6.]

25. In making tactical dispositions, the highest pitch you can attain is to conceal them;

[The piquancy of the paradox evaporates in translation. Concealment is perhaps not so much actual invisibility (see *supra* § 9) as "showing no sign" of what you mean to do, of the plans that are formed in your brain.]

conceal your dispositions, and you will be safe from the prying of the subtlest spies, from the machinations of the wisest brains.

[Tu Mu explains: "Though the enemy may have clever and capable officers, they will not be able to lay any plans against us."]

26. How victory may be produced for them out of the enemy's own tactics—that is what the multitude cannot comprehend.

27. All men can see the tactics whereby I conquer, but what none can see is the strategy out of which victory is evolved.

[I.e., everybody can see superficially how a battle is won; what they cannot see is the long series of plans and combinations which has preceded the battle.]

28. Do not repeat the tactics which have gained you one victory, but let your methods be regulated by the infinite variety of circumstances.

[As Wang Hsi sagely remarks: "There is but one root-principle underlying victory, but the tactics which lead up to it are infinite in number." With this compare Col. Henderson: "The rules of strategy are few and simple. They may be learned in a week. They may be taught by familiar illustrations or a dozen diagrams. But such knowledge will no more teach a man to lead an army like

Napoleon than a knowledge of grammar will teach him to write like Gibbon."]

29. Military tactics are like unto water; for water in its natural course runs away from high places and hastens downwards.

30. So in war, the way is to avoid what is strong and to strike at what is weak.

[Like water, taking the line of least resistance.]

31. Water shapes its course according to the nature of the ground over which it flows; the soldier works out his victory in relation to the foe whom he is facing.

32. Therefore, just as water retains no constant shape, so in warfare there are no constant conditions.

33. He who can modify his tactics in relation to his opponent and thereby succeed in winning, may be called a heaven-born captain.

34. The five elements (water, fire, wood, metal, earth) are not always equally predominant;

[That is, as Wang Hsi says: "they predominate alternately."]

the four seasons make way for each other in turn.

[Literally, "have no invariable seat."]

There are short days and long; the moon has its periods of waning and waxing.

[Cf. V. § 6. The purport of the passage is simply to illustrate the want of fixity in war by the changes constantly taking place in Nature. The comparison is not very happy, however, because the regularity of the phenomena which Sun Tzŭ mentions is by no means paralleled in war.]

CHAPTER 7

Manoeuvering

1. Sun Tzŭ said: In war, the general receives his commands from the sovereign.

2. Having collected an army and concentrated his forces, he must blend and harmonise the different elements thereof before pitching his camp.

[Chang Yu says: "the establishment of harmony and confidence between the higher and lower ranks before venturing into the field;" and he quotes a saying of Wu Tzŭ (chap. 1 ad init.): "Without harmony in the State, no military expedition can be undertaken; without harmony in the army, no battle array can be formed." In an historical romance Sun Tzŭ is represented as saying to Wu Yuan: "As a general rule, those who are waging war should get rid of all the domestic troubles before proceeding to attack the external foe."]

3. After that, comes tactical manoeuvering, than which there is nothing more difficult.

[I have departed slightly from the traditional interpretation of Ts'ao Kung, who says: "From the time of receiving the sovereign's instructions until our encampment over against the enemy, the tactics to be pursued are most difficult." It seems to me that the tactics or manœuvers can hardly be said to begin until the army has sallied forth and encamped, and Ch'ien Hao's note gives color to this view: "For levying, concentrating, harmonizing and entrenching an army, there are plenty of old rules which will serve. The real difficulty comes when we engage in tactical operations." Tu Yu also observes that "the great difficulty is to be beforehand with the enemy in seizing favourable position."]

The difficulty of tactical manoeuvering consists in turning the devious into the direct, and misfortune into gain.

[This sentence contains one of those highly condensed and somewhat enigmatical expressions of which Sun Tzŭ is so fond. This is how it is explained by Ts'ao Kung: "Make it appear that you are a long way off, then cover the distance rapidly and arrive on the scene before your opponent." Tu Mu says: "Hoodwink the enemy, so that he may be remiss and leisurely while you are dashing along with utmost speed." Ho Shih gives a slightly different turn: "Although you may have difficult ground to traverse and natural obstacles to encounter this is a drawback which can be turned into actual advantage by celerity of movement." Signal examples of this saying are afforded by the two famous passages across the Alps—that of Hannibal, which laid Italy at his mercy, and that of Napoleon two thousand years later, which resulted in the great victory of Marengo.]

4. Thus, to take a long and circuitous route, after enticing the enemy out of the way, and though starting after him, to contrive to reach the goal before him, shows knowledge of the artifice of *deviation*.

[Tu Mu cites the famous march of Chao She in 270 B.C. to relieve the town of O-yu, which was closely invested by a Ch'in army. The King of Chao first consulted Lien P'o on the advisability of attempting a relief, but the latter thought the distance too great, and the intervening country too rugged and difficult. His Majesty then turned to Chao She, who fully admitted the hazardous nature of the march, but finally said: "We shall be like two rats fighting in a whole—and the pluckier one will win!" So he left the capital with his army, but had only gone a distance of 30 *li* when he stopped and began throwing up entrenchments. For 28 days he continued strengthening his fortifications, and took care that spies should carry the intelligence to the enemy. The Ch'in general was overjoyed, and attributed his adversary's tardiness to the fact that the beleaguered city was in the Han State, and thus not actually part of Chao territory. But the spies had no sooner departed than Chao She began a forced march lasting for two days and one night, and arrive on the scene of action with such astonishing rapidity that he was able to occupy a commanding position on the "North hill" before the enemy had got wind of his movements. A crushing defeat followed for the Ch'in forces, who were obliged to raise the siege of O-yu in all haste and retreat across the border.]

5. Manoeuvering with an army is advantageous; with an undisciplined multitude, most dangerous.

[I adopt the reading of the *T'ung Tien*, Cheng Yu-hsien and the *T'u Shu*, since they appear to apply the exact nuance required in order to make sense. The commentators using the standard text take this line to mean that manoeuvers may be profitable, or they may be dangerous: it all depends on the ability of the general.]

6. If you set a fully equipped army in march in order to snatch an advantage, the chances are that you will be too late. On the other hand, to detach a flying column for the purpose involves the sacrifice of its baggage and stores.

[Some of the Chinese text is unintelligible to the Chinese commentators, who paraphrase the sentence. I submit my own rendering without much enthusiasm, being convinced that there is some deep-seated corruption in the text. On the whole, it is clear that Sun Tzŭ does not approve of a lengthy march being undertaken without supplies. Cf. infra, § 11.]

7. Thus, if you order your men to roll up their buff-coats, and make forced marches without halting day or night, covering double the usual distance at a stretch,

[The ordinary day's march, according to Tu Mu, was 30 *li*; but on one occasion, when pursuing Liu Pei, Ts'ao Ts'ao is said to have covered the incredible distance of 300 *li* within twenty-four hours.]

doing a hundred *li* in order to wrest an advantage, the leaders of all your three divisions will fall into the hands of the enemy.

8. The stronger men will be in front, the jaded ones will fall behind, and on this plan only one-tenth of your army will reach its destination.

[The moral is, as Ts'ao Kung and others point out: Don't march a hundred *li* to gain a tactical advantage, either with or without impedimenta. Manoeuvers of this description should be confined to short distances. Stonewall Jackson said: "The hardships of forced marches are often more painful than the dangers of battle." He did not often call upon his troops for extraordinary exertions. It was only when he intended a surprise, or when a rapid retreat was imperative, that he sacrificed everything for speed.[1]]

9. If you march fifty *li* in order to outmanoeuver the enemy, you will lose the leader of your first division, and only half your force will reach the goal.

[Literally, "the leader of the first division will be *torn away*."]

10. If you march thirty *li* with the same object, two-thirds of your army will arrive.

[In the *T'ung Tien* is added: "From this we may know the difficulty of manoeuvering."]

---

1. See Col. Henderson, op. cit. vol. I. p. 426.

11. We may take it then that an army without its baggage-train is lost; without provisions it is lost; without bases of supply it is lost.

> [I think Sun Tzŭ meant "stores accumulated in dépôts." But Tu Yu says "fodder and the like," Chang Yu says "Goods in general," and Wang Hsi says "fuel, salt, foodstuffs, etc."]

12. We cannot enter into alliances until we are acquainted with the designs of our neighbours.

13. We are not fit to lead an army on the march unless we are familiar with the face of the country—its mountains and forests, its pitfalls and precipices, its marshes and swamps.

14. We shall be unable to turn natural advantages to account unless we make use of local guides.

> [§§. 12-14 are repeated in chap. XI. § 52.]

15. In war, practise dissimulation, and you will succeed.

> [In the tactics of Turenne, deception of the enemy, especially as to the numerical strength of his troops, took a very prominent position.[2]]

Move only if there is a real advantage to be gained.

16. Whether to concentrate or to divide your troops, must be decided by circumstances.

17. Let your rapidity be that of the wind,

> [The simile is doubly appropriate, because the wind is not only swift but, as Mei Yao-ch'en points out, "invisible and leaves no tracks."]

your compactness that of the forest.

---

2. For a number of maxims on this head, see "Marshal Turenne" (Longmans, 1907), p. 29.

[Meng Shih comes nearer to the mark in his note: "When slowly marching, order and ranks must be preserved"—so as to guard against surprise attacks. But natural forest do not grow in rows, whereas they do generally possess the quality of density or compactness.]

18. In raiding and plundering be like fire,

[Cf. *Shih Ching*, IV. 3. iv. 6: "Fierce as a blazing fire which no man can check."]

in immovability like a mountain.

[That is, when holding a position from which the enemy is trying to dislodge you, or perhaps, as Tu Yu says, when he is trying to entice you into a trap.]

19. Let your plans be dark and impenetrable as night, and when you move, fall like a thunderbolt.

[Tu Yu quotes a saying of T'ai Kung which has passed into a proverb: "You cannot shut your ears to the thunder or your eyes to the lighting—so rapid are they." Likewise, an attack should be made so quickly that it cannot be parried.]

20. When you plunder a countryside, let the spoil be divided amongst your men;

[Sun Tzŭ wishes to lessen the abuses of indiscriminate plundering by insisting that all booty shall be thrown into a common stock, which may afterwards be fairly divided amongst all.]

when you capture new territory, cut it up into allotments for the benefit of the soldiery.

[Ch'en Hao says "quarter your soldiers on the land, and let them sow and plant it." It is by acting on this principle, and harvesting the lands they invaded, that the Chinese have succeeded in carrying out some of their most memorable and triumphant expeditions, such as that of Pan Ch'ao who penetrated to the Caspian, and in more recent years, those of Fu-k'ang-an and Tso Tsung-t'ang.]

21. Ponder and deliberate before you make a move.

[Chang Yu quotes Wei Liao Tzŭ as saying that we must not break camp until we have gained the resisting power of the enemy and the cleverness of the opposing general. Cf. the "seven comparisons" in I. § 13.]

22. He will conquer who has learnt the artifice of deviation.

[See *supra*, §§ 3, 4.]

Such is the art of manoeuvering.

[With these words, the chapter would naturally come to an end. But there now follows a long appendix in the shape of an extract from an earlier book on War, now lost, but apparently extant at the time when Sun Tzŭ wrote. The style of this fragment is not noticeably different from that of Sun Tzŭ himself, but no commentator raises a doubt as to its genuineness.]

23. The Book of Army Management says:

[It is perhaps significant that none of the earlier commentators give us any information about this work. Mei Yao-Ch'en calls it "an ancient military classic," and Wang Hsi, "an old book on war." Considering the enormous amount of fighting that had gone on for centuries before Sun Tzŭ's time between the various kingdoms and principalities of China, it is not in itself improbable that a collection of military maxims should have been made and written down at some earlier period.]

On the field of battle,

[Implied, though not actually in the Chinese.]

the spoken word does not carry far enough: hence the institution of gongs and drums. Nor can ordinary objects be seen clearly enough: hence the institution of banners and flags.

24. Gongs and drums, banners and flags, are means whereby the ears and eyes of the host may be focussed on one particular point.

[Chang Yu says: "If sight and hearing converge simultaneously on the same object, the evolutions of as many as a million soldiers will be like those of a single man."!]

25. The host thus forming a single united body, is it impossible either for the brave to advance alone, or for the cowardly to retreat alone.

[Chuang Yu quotes a saying: "Equally guilty are those who advance against orders and those who retreat against orders." Tu Mu tells a story in this connection of Wu Ch'i, when he was fighting against the Ch'in State. Before the battle had begun, one of his soldiers, a man of matchless daring, sallied forth by himself, captured two heads from the enemy, and returned to camp. Wu Ch'i had the man instantly executed, whereupon an officer ventured to remonstrate, saying: "This man was a good soldier, and ought not to have been beheaded." Wu Ch'i replied: "I fully believe he was a good soldier, but I had him beheaded because he acted without orders."]

This is the art of handling large masses of men.

26. In night-fighting, then, make much use of signal-fires and drums, and in fighting by day, of flags and banners, as a means of influencing the ears and eyes of your army.

[Ch'en Hao alludes to Li Kuang-pi's night ride to Ho-yang at the head of 500 mounted men; they made such an imposing display with torches, that though the rebel leader Shih Ssu-ming had a large army, he did not dare to dispute their passage.]

27. A whole army may be robbed of its spirit;

["In war," says Chang Yu, "if a spirit of anger can be made to pervade all ranks of an army at one and the same time, its onset will be irresistible. Now the spirit of the enemy's soldiers will be keenest when they have newly arrived on the scene, and it is therefore our cue not to fight at once, but to wait until their ardor and enthusiasm have worn off, and then strike. It is in this way that they may be robbed of their keen spirit." Li Ch'uan and others tell an anecdote (to be found in the *Tso Chuan*, year 10, § 1) of Ts'ao Kuei, a protege of Duke Chuang of Lu. The latter State was attacked by Ch'i, and the duke was about to join battle at Ch'ang-cho, after the first roll of the enemy's drums, when Ts'ao said: "Not just yet." Only after their drums had beaten for the third time, did he give the word for attack. Then they fought, and the men of Ch'i were utterly defeated. Questioned afterwards by the Duke as to the meaning of his delay, Ts'ao Kuei replied: "In battle, a courageous spirit is everything. Now the first roll of the drum tends to create this spirit, but with the second it is already on the wane, and after the third it is gone altogether. I attacked when their spirit was gone and ours was at its height. Hence our victory." Wu Tzŭ (chap. 4) puts "spirit" first among the "four important influences" in war, and continues: "The value of a whole army—a mighty host of a million men—is dependent on one man alone: such is the influence of spirit!"]

a commander-in-chief may be robbed of his presence of mind.

[Chang Yu says: "Presence of mind is the general's most important asset. It is the quality which enables him to discipline disorder and to inspire courage into the panic-stricken." The great general Li Ching (A.D. 571-649) has a saying: "Attacking does not merely consist in assaulting walled cities or striking at an army in battle array; it must include the art of assailing the enemy's mental equilibrium."]

28. Now a soldier's spirit is keenest in the morning;

[Always provided, I suppose, that he has had breakfast. At the battle of the Trebia, the Romans were foolishly allowed to fight fasting, whereas Hannibal's men had breakfasted at their leisure. See Livy, XXI, liv. 8, lv. 1 and 8.]

by noonday it has begun to flag; and in the evening, his mind is bent only on returning to camp.

29. A clever general, therefore, avoids an army when its spirit is keen, but attacks it when it is sluggish and inclined to return. This is the art of studying moods.

30. Disciplined and calm, to await the appearance of disorder and hubbub amongst the enemy:—this is the art of retaining self-possession.

31. To be near the goal while the enemy is still far from it, to wait at ease while the enemy is toiling and struggling, to be well-fed while the enemy is famished:—this is the art of husbanding one's strength.

32. To refrain from intercepting an enemy whose banners are in perfect order, to refrain from attacking an army drawn up in calm and confident array:—this is the art of studying circumstances.

33. It is a military axiom not to advance uphill against the enemy, nor to oppose him when he comes downhill.

34. Do not pursue an enemy who simulates flight; do not attack soldiers whose temper is keen.

35. Do not swallow a bait offered by the enemy.

> [Li Ch'uan and Tu Mu, with extraordinary inability to see a metaphor, take these words quite literally of food and drink that have been poisoned by the enemy. Ch'en Hao and Chang Yu carefully point out that the saying has a wider application.]

Do not interfere with an army that is returning home.

> [The commentators explain this rather singular piece of advice by saying that a man whose heart is set on returning home will fight to the death against any attempt to bar his way, and is therefore too dangerous an opponent to be tackled. Chang Yu quotes the words of Han Hsin: "Invincible is the soldier who hath his desire and returneth homewards." A marvelous tale is told of Ts'ao

Ts'ao's courage and resource in ch. 1 of the *San Kuo Chi*, In 198 A.D., he was besieging Chang Hsiu in Jang, when Liu Piao sent reinforcements with a view to cutting off Ts'ao's retreat. The latter was obliged to draw off his troops, only to find himself hemmed in between two enemies, who were guarding each outlet of a narrow pass in which he had engaged himself. In this desperate plight Ts'ao waited until nightfall, when he bored a tunnel into the mountain side and laid an ambush in it. As soon as the whole army had passed by, the hidden troops fell on his rear, while Ts'ao himself turned and met his pursuers in front, so that they were thrown into confusion and annihilated. Ts'ao Ts'ao said afterwards: "The brigands tried to check my army in its retreat and brought me to battle in a desperate position: hence I knew how to overcome them."]

36. When you surround an army, leave an outlet free.

[This does not mean that the enemy is to be allowed to escape. The object, as Tu Mu puts it, is "to make him believe that there is a road to safety, and thus prevent his fighting with the courage of despair." Tu Mu adds pleasantly: "After that, you may crush him."]

Do not press a desperate foe too hard.

[Ch'en Hao quotes the saying: "Birds and beasts when brought to bay will use their claws and teeth." Chang Yu says: "If your adversary has burned his boats and destroyed his cooking-pots, and is ready to stake all on the issue of a battle, he must not be pushed to extremities." Ho Shih illustrates the meaning by a story taken from the life of Yen-ch'ing. That general, together with his colleague Tu Chung-wei was surrounded by a vastly superior army of Khitans in the year 945 A.D. The country was bare and desert-like, and the little Chinese force was soon in dire straits for want of water. The wells they bored ran dry, and the men were reduced to squeezing lumps of mud and sucking out the moisture. Their ranks thinned rapidly, until at last Fu Yen-ch'ing exclaimed: "We are desperate men. Far better to die for our country than to go with fettered hands into captivity!" A strong gale happened to be blowing from the northeast and darkening the air with dense clouds of sandy dust. To Chung-wei was for waiting until this had abated before deciding on a final attack; but luckily another officer, Li Shou-cheng by name, was quicker to see an opportunity, and said: "They are many and we are few, but in the midst of this sandstorm our numbers will not be discernible; victory will go to the strenuous fighter, and the wind will be our best ally." Accordingly, Fu Yen-ch'ing made a sudden and wholly unexpected onslaught with his cavalry, routed the barbarians and succeeded in breaking through to safety.]

37. Such is the art of warfare.

CHAPTER 8

Variation of Tactics

[The heading means literally "The Nine Variations," but as Sun Tzŭ does not appear to enumerate these, and as, indeed, he has already told us (V §§ 6-11) that such deflections from the ordinary course are practically innumerable, we have little option but to follow Wang Hsi, who says that "Nine" stands for an indefinitely large number. "All it means is that in warfare we ought to vary our tactics to the utmost degree.... I do not know what Ts'ao Kung makes these Nine Variations out to be, but it has been suggested that they are connected with the Nine Situations"– of chapt. XI. This is the view adopted by Chang Yu. The only other alternative is to suppose that something has been lost—a supposition to which the unusual shortness of the chapter lends some weight.]

1. Sun Tzŭ said: In war, the general receives his commands from the sovereign, collects his army and concentrates his forces.

[Repeated from VII. § 1, where it is certainly more in place. It may have been interpolated here merely in order to supply a beginning to the chapter.]

2. When in difficult country, do not encamp. In country where high roads intersect, join hands with your allies. Do not linger in dangerously isolated positions.

[The last situation is not one of the Nine Situations as given in the beginning of chap. XI, but occurs later on (ibid. § 43. q.v.). Chang Yu defines this situation as being situated across the frontier, in hostile territory. Li Ch'uan says it is "country in which there are no springs or wells, flocks or herds, vegetables or firewood;" Chia Lin, "one of gorges, chasms and precipices, without a road by which to advance."]

In hemmed-in situations, you must resort to stratagem. In a desperate position, you must fight.

3. There are roads which must not be followed,

["Especially those leading through narrow defiles," says Li Ch'uan, "where an ambush is to be feared."]

armies which must be not attacked,

[More correctly, perhaps, "there are times when an army must not be attacked." Ch'en Hao says: "When you see your way to obtain a rival advantage, but are powerless to inflict a real defeat, refrain from attacking, for fear of overtaxing your men's strength."]

towns which must not be besieged,

[Cf. III. § 4 Ts'ao Kung gives an interesting illustration from his own experience. When invading the territory of Hsu-chou, he ignored the city of Hua-pi, which lay directly in his path, and pressed on into the heart of the country. This excellent strategy was rewarded by the subsequent capture of no fewer than fourteen important district cities. Chang Yu says: "No town should be attacked which, if taken, cannot be held, or if left alone, will not cause any trouble." Hsun Ying, when urged to attack Pi-yang, replied: "The city is small and well-fortified; even if I succeed intaking it, it will be no great feat of arms; whereas if I fail, I shall make myself a laughing-stock." In the seventeenth century, sieges still formed a large proportion of war. It was Turenne who directed attention to the importance of marches, countermarches and manœuvers. He said: "It is a great mistake to waste men in taking a town when the same expenditure of soldiers will gain a province."[1]]

positions which must not be contested, commands of the sovereign which must not be obeyed.

[This is a hard saying for the Chinese, with their reverence for authority, and Wei Liao Tzŭ (quoted by Tu Mu) is moved to exclaim: "Weapons are baleful instruments, strife is antagonistic to virtue, a military commander is the negation of civil order!" The unpalatable fact remains, however, that even Imperial wishes must be subordinated to military necessity.]

4. The general who thoroughly understands the advantages that accompany variation of tactics knows how to handle his troops.

5. The general who does not understand these, may be well acquainted with the configuration of the country, yet he will not be able to turn his knowledge to practical account.

[Literally, "get the advantage of the ground," which means not only securing good positions, but availing oneself of natural advantages in every possible way. Chang Yu says: "Every kind of ground is characterized by certain natural features, and also gives scope for a certain variability of plan. How it is possible to turn these natural features to account unless topographical knowledge is supplemented by versatility of mind?"]

6. So, the student of war who is unversed in the art of war of varying his plans, even though he be acquainted with the Five Advantages, will fail to make the best use of his men.

---

1. "Marshal Turenne," p. 50.

[Chia Lin tells us that these imply five obvious and generally advantageous lines of action, namely: "if a certain road is short, it must be followed; if an army is isolated, it must be attacked; if a town is in a parlous condition, it must be besieged; if a position can be stormed, it must be attempted; and if consistent with military operations, the ruler's commands must be obeyed." But there are circumstances which sometimes forbid a general to use these advantages. For instance, "a certain road may be the shortest way for him, but if he knows that it abounds in natural obstacles, or that the enemy has laid an ambush on it, he will not follow that road. A hostile force may be open to attack, but if he knows that it is hard-pressed and likely to fight with desperation, he will refrain from striking," and so on.]

7. Hence in the wise leader's plans, considerations of advantage and of disadvantage will be blended together.

["Whether in an advantageous position or a disadvantageous one," says Ts'ao Kung, "the opposite state should be always present to your mind."]

8. If our expectation of advantage be tempered in this way, we may succeed in accomplishing the essential part of our schemes.

[Tu Mu says: "If we wish to wrest an advantage from the enemy, we must not fix our minds on that alone, but allow for the possibility of the enemy also doing some harm to us, and let this enter as a factor into our calculations."]

9. If, on the other hand, in the midst of difficulties we are always ready to seize an advantage, we may extricate ourselves from misfortune.

[Tu Mu says: "If I wish to extricate myself from a dangerous position, I must consider not only the enemy's ability to injure me, but also my own ability to gain an advantage over the enemy. If in my counsels these two considerations are properly blended, I shall succeed in liberating myself.... For instance; if I am surrounded by the enemy and only think of effecting an escape, the nervelessness of my policy will incite my adversary to pursue and crush me; it would be far better to encourage my men to deliver a bold counter-attack, and use the advantage thus gained to free myself from the enemy's toils." See the story of Ts'ao Ts'ao, VII. § 35, note.]

10. Reduce the hostile chiefs by inflicting damage on them;

[Chia Lin enumerates several ways of inflicting this injury, some of which would only occur to the Oriental mind:—"Entice away the enemy's best and wisest men, so that he may be left without counselors. Introduce traitors into his country, that the government policy may be rendered futile. Foment intrigue and deceit, and thus sow dissension between the ruler and his ministers. By means of every artful contrivance, cause deterioration amongst his men and waste of his treasure. Corrupt his morals by insidious gifts leading him into excess. Disturb and unsettle his mind by presenting him with lovely women." Chang Yu (after Wang Hsi) makes a different interpretation of Sun Tzŭ here: "Get the enemy into a position where he must suffer injury, and he will submit of his own accord."]

and make trouble for them,

[Tu Mu, in this phrase, in his interpretation indicates that trouble should be made for the enemy affecting their "possessions," or, as we might say, "assets," which he considers to be "a large army, a rich exchequer, harmony amongst the soldiers, punctual fulfillment of commands." These give us a whip-hand over the enemy.]

and keep them constantly engaged;

[Literally, "make servants of them." Tu Yu says "prevent them from having any rest."]

hold out specious allurements, and make them rush to any given point.

[Meng Shih's note contains an excellent example of the idiomatic use of: "cause them to forget *pien* (the reasons for acting otherwise than on their first impulse), and hasten in our direction."]

11. The art of war teaches us to rely not on the likelihood of the enemy's not coming, but on our own readiness to receive him; not on the chance of his not attacking, but rather on the fact that we have made our position unassailable.

12. There are five dangerous faults which may affect a general: (1) Recklessness, which leads to destruction;

["Bravery without forethought," as Ts'ao Kung analyzes it, which causes a man to fight blindly and desperately like a mad bull. Such an opponent, says Chang Yu, "must not be encountered with brute force, but may be lured into an ambush and slain." Cf. Wu Tzŭ, chap. IV. ad init.: "In estimating the character of a general, men are wont to pay exclusive attention to his courage, forgetting that courage is only one out of many qualities which a general should possess. The merely brave man is prone to fight recklessly; and he who fights recklessly, without any perception of what is expedient, must be condemned." Ssu-ma Fa, too, makes the incisive remark: "Simply going to one's death does not bring about victory."]

(2) cowardice, which leads to capture;

[Ts'ao Kung defines the Chinese word translated here as "cowardice" as being of the man "whom timidity prevents from advancing to seize an advantage," and Wang Hsi adds "who is quick to flee at the sight of danger." Meng Shih gives the closer paraphrase "he who is bent on returning alive," this is, the man who will never take a risk. But, as Sun Tzŭ knew, nothing is to be achieved in war unless you are willing to take risks. T'ai Kung said: "He who lets an advantage slip will subsequently bring upon himself real disaster." In 404 A.D., Liu Yu pursued the rebel Huan Hsuan up the Yangtsze and fought a naval battle with him at the island of Ch'eng-hung. The loyal troops numbered only a few thousands, while their opponents were in great force. But Huan Hsuan, fearing the fate which was in store for him should be be overcome, had a light boat made fast to the side of his war-junk, so that he might escape, if necessary, at a moment's notice. The natural result was that the fighting spirit of his soldiers was utterly quenched, and when the loyalists made an attack from windward with fireships, all striving with the utmost ardor to be first in the fray, Huan Hsuan's forces were routed, had to burn all their baggage and fled for two days and nights without stopping. Chang Yu tells a somewhat similar story of Chao Ying-ch'i, a general of the Chin State who during a battle with the army of Ch'u in 597 B.C. had a boat kept in readiness for him on the river, wishing in case of defeat to be the first to get across.]

(3) a hasty temper, which can be provoked by insults;

[Tu Mu tells us that Yao Hsing, when opposed in 357 A.D. by Huang Mei, Teng Ch'iang and others shut himself up behind his walls and refused to fight. Teng Ch'iang said: "Our adversary is of a choleric temper and easily provoked; let us make constant sallies and break down his walls, then he will grow angry and come out. Once we can bring his force to battle, it is doomed to be our prey." This plan was acted upon, Yao Hsiang came out to fight, was lured as far as San-yuan by the enemy's pretended flight, and finally attacked and slain.]

(4) a delicacy of honour which is sensitive to shame;

[This need not be taken to mean that a sense of honour is really a defect in a general. What Sun Tzŭ condemns is rather an exaggerated sensitiveness to slanderous reports, the thin-skinned man who is stung by opprobrium, however undeserved. Mei Yao-ch'en truly observes, though somewhat paradoxically: "The seeker after glory should be careless of public opinion."]

(5) over-solicitude for his men, which exposes him to worry and trouble.

[Here again, Sun Tzŭ does not mean that the general is to be careless of the welfare of his troops. All he wishes to emphasize is the danger of sacrificing any important military advantage to the immediate comfort of his men. This is a shortsighted policy, because in the long run the troops will suffer more from the defeat, or, at best, the prolongation of the war, which will be the consequence. A mistaken feeling of pity will often induce a general to relieve a beleaguered city, or to reinforce a hard-pressed detachment, contrary to his military instincts. It is now generally admitted that our repeated efforts to relieve Ladysmith in the South African War were so many strategical blunders which defeated their own purpose. And in the end, relief came through the very man who started out with the distinct resolve no longer to subordinate the interests of the whole to sentiment in favour of a part. An old soldier of one of our generals who failed most conspicuously in this war, tried once, I remember, to defend him to me on the ground that he was always "so good to his men." By this plea, had he but known it, he was only condemning him out of Sun Tzŭ's mouth.]

13. These are the five besetting sins of a general, ruinous to the conduct of war.

14. When an army is overthrown and its leader slain, the cause will surely be found among these five dangerous faults. Let them be a subject of meditation.

CHAPTER 9

The Army on the March

[The contents of this interesting chapter are better indicated in § 1 than by this heading.]

1. Sun Tzŭ said: We come now to the question of encamping the army, and observing signs of the enemy. Pass quickly over mountains, and keep in the neighbourhood of valleys.

[The idea is, not to linger among barren uplands, but to keep close to supplies of water and grass. Cf. Wu Tzŭ, ch. 3: "Abide not in natural ovens," i.e. "the openings of valleys." Chang Yu tells the following anecdote: "Wu-tu Ch'iang was a robber captain in the time of the Later Han, and Ma Yuan was sent to exterminate his gang. Ch'iang having found a refuge in the hills, Ma Yuan made no attempt to force a battle, but seized all the favourable positions commanding supplies of water and forage. Ch'iang was soon in such a desperate plight for want of provisions that he was forced to make a total surrender. He did not know the advantage of keeping in the neighbourhood of valleys."]

2. Camp in high places,

[Not on high hills, but on knolls or hillocks elevated above the surrounding country.]

facing the sun.

[Tu Mu takes this to mean "facing south," and Ch'en Hao "facing east." Cf. infra, §§ 11, 13.]

Do not climb heights in order to fight. So much for mountain warfare.

3. After crossing a river, you should get far away from it.

["In order to tempt the enemy to cross after you," according to Ts'ao Kung, and also, says Chang Yu, "in order not to be impeded in your evolutions." The *T'ung Tien* reads, "If *the enemy* crosses a river," etc. But in view of the next sentence, this is almost certainly an interpolation.]

4. When an invading force crosses a river in its onward march, do not advance to meet it in mid-stream. It will be best to let half the army get across, and then deliver your attack.

[Li Ch'uan alludes to the great victory won by Han Hsin over Lung Chu at the Wei River. Turning to the *Ch'ien Han Shu*, ch. 34, fol. 6 verso, we find the battle described as follows: "The two armies were drawn up on opposite sides of the river. In the night, Han Hsin ordered his men to take some ten thousand sacks filled with sand and construct a dam higher up. Then, leading half his army across, he attacked Lung Chu; but after a time, pretending to have failed in his attempt, he hastily withdrew to the other bank. Lung Chu was much elated by this unlooked-for success, and exclaiming: "I felt sure that Han Hsin was really a coward!" he pursued him and began crossing the river in his turn. Han Hsin now sent a party to cut open the sandbags, thus releasing a great volume of water, which swept down and prevented the greater portion of Lung Chu's army from getting across. He then turned upon the force which had been cut off, and annihilated it, Lung Chu himself being amongst the slain. The rest of the army, on the further bank, also scattered and fled in all directions."]

5. If you are anxious to fight, you should not go to meet the invader near a river which he has to cross.

[For fear of preventing his crossing.]

6. Moor your craft higher up than the enemy, and facing the sun.

[See *supra*, § 2. The repetition of these words in connection with water is very awkward. Chang Yu has the note: "Said either of troops marshalled on the river-bank, or of boats anchored in the stream itself; in either case it is essential to be higher than the enemy and facing the sun." The other commentators are not at all explicit.]

Do not move up-stream to meet the enemy.

[Tu Mu says: "As water flows downwards, we must not pitch our camp on the lower reaches of a river, for fear the enemy should open the sluices and sweep us away in a flood. Chu-ko Wu-hou has remarked that 'in river warfare we must not advance against the stream,' which is as much as to say that our fleet must not be anchored below that of the enemy, for then they would be able to take advantage of the current and make short work of us." There is also the danger, noted by other commentators, that the enemy may throw poison on the water to be carried down to us.]

So much for river warfare.

7. In crossing salt-marshes, your sole concern should be to get over them quickly, without any delay.

[Because of the lack of fresh water, the poor quality of the herbage, and last but not least, because they are low, flat, and exposed to attack.]

8. If forced to fight in a salt-marsh, you should have water and grass near you, and get your back to a clump of trees.

[Li Ch'uan remarks that the ground is less likely to be treacherous where there are trees, while Tu Mu says that they will serve to protect the rear.]

So much for operations in salt-marshes.

9. In dry, level country, take up an easily accessible position with rising ground to your right and on your rear,

[Tu Mu quotes T'ai Kung as saying: "An army should have a stream or a marsh on its left, and a hill or tumulus on its right."]

so that the danger may be in front, and safety lie behind. So much for campaigning in flat country.

10. These are the four useful branches of military knowledge

[Those, namely, concerned with (1) mountains, (2) rivers, (3) marshes, and (4) plains. Compare Napoleon's "Military Maxims," no. 1.]

which enabled the Yellow Emperor to vanquish four several sovereigns.

[Regarding the "Yellow Emperor": Mei Yao-ch'en asks, with some plausibility, whether there is an error in the text as nothing is known of Huang Ti having conquered four other Emperors. The *Shih Chi* (ch. 1 ad init.) speaks only of his victories over Yen Ti and Ch'ih Yu. In the *Liu T'ao* it is mentioned that he "fought seventy battles and pacified the Empire." Ts'ao Kung's explanation is, that the Yellow Emperor was the first to institute the feudal system of vassals princes, each of whom (to the number of four) originally bore the title of Emperor. Li Ch'uan tells us that the art of war originated under Huang Ti, who received it from his Minister Feng Hou.]

11. All armies prefer high ground to low,

["High Ground," says Mei Yao-ch'en, "is not only more agreeable and salubrious, but more convenient from a military point of view; low ground is not only damp and unhealthy, but also disadvantageous for fighting."]

and sunny places to dark.

12. If you are careful of your men,

[Ts'ao Kung says: "Make for fresh water and pasture, where you can turn out your animals to graze."]

and camp on hard ground, the army will be free from disease of every kind,

[Chang Yu says: "The dryness of the climate will prevent the outbreak of illness."]

and this will spell victory.

13. When you come to a hill or a bank, occupy the sunny side, with the slope on your right rear. Thus you will at once act for the benefit of your soldiers and utilise the natural advantages of the ground.

14. When, in consequence of heavy rains up-country, a river which you wish to ford is swollen and flecked with foam, you must wait until it subsides.

15. Country in which there are precipitous cliffs with torrents running between, deep natural hollows,

[The latter defined as "places enclosed on every side by steep banks, with pools of water at the bottom."]

confined places,

[Defined as "natural pens or prisons" or "places surrounded by precipices on three sides—easy to get into, but hard to get out of."]

tangled thickets,

[Defined as "places covered with such dense undergrowth that spears cannot be used."]

quagmires

> [Defined as "low-lying places, so heavy with mud as to be impassable for chariots and horsemen."]

and crevasses,

> [Defined by Mei Yao-ch'en as "a narrow difficult way between beetling cliffs." Tu Mu's note is "ground covered with trees and rocks, and intersected by numerous ravines and pitfalls." This is very vague, but Chia Lin explains it clearly enough as a defile or narrow pass, and Chang Yu takes much the same view. On the whole, the weight of the commentators certainly inclines to the rendering "defile." But the ordinary meaning of the Chinese in one place is "a crack or fissure" and the fact that the meaning of the Chinese elsewhere in the sentence indicates something in the nature of a defile, make me think that Sun Tzŭ is here speaking of crevasses.]

should be left with all possible speed and not approached.

16. While we keep away from such places, we should get the enemy to approach them; while we face them, we should let the enemy have them on his rear.

17. If in the neighbourhood of your camp there should be any hilly country, ponds surrounded by aquatic grass, hollow basins filled with reeds, or woods with thick undergrowth, they must be carefully routed out and searched; for these are places where men in ambush or insidious spies are likely to be lurking.

> [Chang Yu has the note: "We must also be on our guard against traitors who may lie in close covert, secretly spying out our weaknesses and overhearing our instructions."]

18. When the enemy is close at hand and remains quiet, he is relying on the natural strength of his position.

> [Here begin Sun Tzŭ's remarks on the reading of signs, much of

which is so good that it could almost be included in a modern manual like Gen. Baden-Powell's "Aids to Scouting."]

19. When he keeps aloof and tries to provoke a battle, he is anxious for the other side to advance.

[Probably because we are in a strong position from which he wishes to dislodge us. "If he came close up to us, says Tu Mu, "and tried to force a battle, he would seem to despise us, and there would be less probability of our responding to the challenge."]

20. If his place of encampment is easy of access, he is tendering a bait.

21. Movement amongst the trees of a forest shows that the enemy is advancing.

[Ts'ao Kung explains this as "felling trees to clear a passage," and Chang Yu says: "Every man sends out scouts to climb high places and observe the enemy. If a scout sees that the trees of a forest are moving and shaking, he may know that they are being cut down to clear a passage for the enemy's march."]

The appearance of a number of screens in the midst of thick grass means that the enemy wants to make us suspicious.

[Tu Yu's explanation, borrowed from Ts'ao Kung's, is as follows: "The presence of a number of screens or sheds in the midst of thick vegetation is a sure sign that the enemy has fled and, fearing pursuit, has constructed these hiding-places in order to make us suspect an ambush." It appears that these "screens" were hastily knotted together out of any long grass which the retreating enemy happened to come across.]

22. The rising of birds in their flight is the sign of an ambuscade.

[Chang Yu's explanation is doubtless right: "When birds that are flying along in a straight line suddenly shoot upwards, it means that soldiers are in ambush at the spot beneath."]

Startled beasts indicate that a sudden attack is coming.

23. When there is dust rising in a high column, it is the sign of chariots advancing; when the dust is low, but spread over a wide area, it betokens the approach of infantry.

["High and sharp," or rising to a peak, is of course somewhat exaggerated as applied to dust. The commentators explain the phenomenon by saying that horses and chariots, being heavier than men, raise more dust, and also follow one another in the same wheel-track, whereas foot-soldiers would be marching in ranks, many abreast. According to Chang Yu, "every army on the march must have scouts some way in advance, who on sighting dust raised by the enemy, will gallop back and report it to the commander-in-chief." Cf. Gen. Baden-Powell: "As you move along, say, in a hostile country, your eyes should be looking afar for the enemy or any signs of him: figures, dust rising, birds getting up, glitter of arms, etc."[1]]

When it branches out in different directions, it shows that parties have been sent to collect firewood. A few clouds of dust moving to and fro signify that the army is encamping.

[Chang Yu says: "In apportioning the defences for a cantonment, light horse will be sent out to survey the position and ascertain the weak and strong points all along its circumference. Hence the small quantity of dust and its motion."]

24. Humble words and increased preparations are signs that the enemy is about to advance.

["As though they stood in great fear of us," says Tu Mu. "Their object is to make us contemptuous and careless, after which they will attack us." Chang Yu alludes to the story of T'ien Tan of the Ch'i-mo against the Yen forces, led by Ch'i Chieh. In ch. 82 of the *Shih Chi* we read: "T'ien Tan openly said: 'My only fear is that the Yen army may cut off the noses of their Ch'i prisoners

---

1. "Aids to Scouting," p. 26.

and place them in the front rank to fight against us; that would be the undoing of our city.' The other side being informed of this speech, at once acted on the suggestion; but those within the city were enraged at seeing their fellow-countrymen thus mutilated, and fearing only lest they should fall into the enemy's hands, were nerved to defend themselves more obstinately than ever. Once again T'ien Tan sent back converted spies who reported these words to the enemy: "What I dread most is that the men of Yen may dig up the ancestral tombs outside the town, and by inflicting this indignity on our forefathers cause us to become faint-hearted.' Forthwith the besiegers dug up all the graves and burned the corpses lying in them. And the inhabitants of Chi-mo, witnessing the outrage from the city-walls, wept passionately and were all impatient to go out and fight, their fury being increased tenfold. T'ien Tan knew then that his soldiers were ready for any enterprise. But instead of a sword, he himself took a mattock in his hands, and ordered others to be distributed amongst his best warriors, while the ranks were filled up with their wives and concubines. He then served out all the remaining rations and bade his men eat their fill. The regular soldiers were told to keep out of sight, and the walls were manned with the old and weaker men and with women. This done, envoys were dispatched to the enemy's camp to arrange terms of surrender, whereupon the Yen army began shouting for joy. T'ien Tan also collected 20,000 ounces of silver from the people, and got the wealthy citizens of Chi-mo to send it to the Yen general with the prayer that, when the town capitulated, he would not allow their homes to be plundered or their women to be maltreated. Ch'i Chieh, in high good humor, granted their prayer; but his army now became increasingly slack and careless. Meanwhile, T'ien Tan got together a thousand oxen, decked them with pieces of red silk, painted their bodies, dragon-like, with colored stripes, and fastened sharp blades on their horns and well-greased rushes on their tails. When night came on, he lighted the ends of the rushes, and drove the oxen through a number of holes which he had pierced in the walls, backing them up with a force of 5000 picked warriors. The animals, maddened with pain, dashed furiously into the enemy's camp where they caused the utmost confusion and dismay; for their tails acted as torches, showing up the hideous pattern on their bodies, and the weapons on their horns killed or wounded any with whom they came into contact. In the meantime, the band of 5000 had crept up with gags in their mouths, and now threw themselves on the enemy. At the same moment a frightful din arose in the city itself, all those that remained behind making as much noise as possible by banging drums and hammering on bronze vessels, until heaven and earth were convulsed by the uproar. Terror-stricken, the Yen army fled in disorder, hotly pursued by the men of Ch'i, who succeeded in slaying their general Ch'i Chien.... The result of the battle was the ultimate recovery of some seventy cities which had belonged to the Ch'i State."]

Violent language and driving forward as if to the attack are signs that he will retreat.

25. When the light chariots come out first and take up a position on the wings, it is a sign that the enemy is forming for battle.

26. Peace proposals unaccompanied by a sworn covenant indicate a plot.

[The reading here is uncertain. Li Ch'uan indicates "a treaty confirmed by oaths and hostages." Wang Hsi and Chang Yu, on the other hand, simply say "without reason," "on a frivolous pretext."]

27. When there is much running about

[Every man hastening to his proper place under his own regimental banner.]

and the soldiers fall into rank, it means that the critical moment has come.

28. When some are seen advancing and some retreating, it is a lure.

29. When the soldiers stand leaning on their spears, they are faint from want of food.

30. If those who are sent to draw water begin by drinking themselves, the army is suffering from thirst.

[As Tu Mu remarks: "One may know the condition of a whole army from the behavior of a single man."]

31. If the enemy sees an advantage to be gained and makes no effort to secure it, the soldiers are exhausted.

32. If birds gather on any spot, it is unoccupied.

[A useful fact to bear in mind when, for instance, as Ch'en Hao says, the enemy has secretly abandoned his camp.]

Clamour by night betokens nervousness.

33. If there is disturbance in the camp, the general's authority is weak. If the banners and flags are shifted about, sedition is afoot. If the officers are angry, it means that the men are weary.

[Tu Mu understands the sentence differently: "If all the officers of an army are angry with their general, it means that they are broken with fatigue" owing to the exertions which he has demanded from them.]

34. When an army feeds its horses with grain and kills its cattle for food,

[In the ordinary course of things, the men would be fed on grain and the horses chiefly on grass.]

and when the men do not hang their cooking-pots over the camp-fires, showing that they will not return to their tents, you may know that they are determined to fight to the death.

[I may quote here the illustrative passage from the *Hou Han Shu*, ch. 71, given in abbreviated form by the *P'ei Wen Yun Fu:* "The rebel

Wang Kuo of Liang was besieging the town of Ch'en-ts'ang, and Huang-fu Sung, who was in supreme command, and Tung Cho were sent out against him. The latter pressed for hasty measures, but Sung turned a deaf ear to his counsel. At last the rebels were utterly worn out, and began to throw down their weapons of their own accord. Sung was not advancing to the attack, but Cho said: 'It is a principle of war not to pursue desperate men and not to press a retreating host.' Sung answered: 'That does not apply here. What I am about to attack is a jaded army, not a retreating host; with disciplined troops I am falling on a disorganized multitude, not a band of desperate men.' Thereupon he advances to the attack unsupported by his colleague, and routed the enemy, Wang Kuo being slain."]

35. The sight of men whispering together in small knots or speaking in subdued tones points to disaffection amongst the rank and file.

36. Too frequent rewards signify that the enemy is at the end of his resources;

[Because, when an army is hard pressed, as Tu Mu says, there is always a fear of mutiny, and lavish rewards are given to keep the men in good temper.]

too many punishments betray a condition of dire distress.

[Because in such case discipline becomes relaxed, and unwonted severity is necessary to keep the men to their duty.]

37. To begin by bluster, but afterwards to take fright at the enemy's numbers, shows a supreme lack of intelligence.

[I follow the interpretation of Ts'ao Kung, also adopted by Li Ch'uan, Tu Mu, and Chang Yu. Another possible meaning set forth by Tu Yu, Chia Lin, Mei Tao-ch'en and Wang Hsi, is: "The general who is first tyrannical towards his men, and then in terror lest they should mutiny, etc." This would connect the sentence with what went before about rewards and punishments.]

38. When envoys are sent with compliments in their mouths, it is a sign that the enemy wishes for a truce.

[Tu Mu says: "If the enemy open friendly relations be sending hostages, it is a sign that they are anxious for an armistice, either because their strength is exhausted or for some other reason." But it hardly needs a Sun Tzŭ to draw such an obvious inference.]

39. If the enemy's troops march up angrily and remain facing ours for a long time without either joining battle or taking themselves off again, the situation is one that demands great vigilance and circumspection.

[Ts'ao Kung says a manoeuver of this sort may be only a ruse to gain time for an unexpected flank attack or the laying of an ambush.]

40. If our troops are no more in number than the enemy, that is amply sufficient; it only means that no direct attack can be made.

[Literally, "no martial advance." That is to say, *cheng* tactics and frontal attacks must be eschewed, and stratagem resorted to instead.]

What we can do is simply to concentrate all our available strength, keep a close watch on the enemy, and obtain reinforcements.

[This is an obscure sentence, and none of the commentators succeed in squeezing very good sense out of it. I follow Li Ch'uan, who appears to offer the simplest explanation: "Only the side that gets more men will win." Fortunately we have Chang Yu to expound its meaning to us in language which is lucidity itself: "When the numbers are even, and no favourable opening presents itself, although we may not be strong enough to deliver a sustained attack, we can find additional recruits amongst our sutlers and camp-followers, and then, concentrating our forces and keeping a close watch on the enemy, contrive to snatch the victory. But we must avoid borrowing foreign soldiers to help us." He then quotes from Wei Liao Tzŭ, ch. 3: "The nominal strength of mercenary troops may be 100,000, but their real value will be not more than half that figure."]

41. He who exercises no forethought but makes light of his opponents is sure to be captured by them.

> [Ch'en Hao, quoting from the *Tso Chuan*, says: "If bees and scorpions carry poison, how much more will a hostile state! Even a puny opponent, then, should not be treated with contempt."]

42. If soldiers are punished before they have grown attached to you, they will not prove submissive; and, unless submissive, then will be practically useless. If, when the soldiers have become attached to you, punishments are not enforced, they will still be useless.

43. Therefore soldiers must be treated in the first instance with humanity, but kept under control by means of iron discipline.

> [Yen Tzŭ [B.C. 493] said of Ssu-ma Jang-chu: "His civil virtues endeared him to the people; his martial prowess kept his enemies in awe." Cf. Wu Tzŭ, ch. 4 init.: "The ideal commander unites culture with a warlike temper; the profession of arms requires a combination of hardness and tenderness."]

This is a certain road to victory.

44. If in training soldiers commands are habitually enforced, the army will be well-disciplined; if not, its discipline will be bad.

45. If a general shows confidence in his men but always insists on his orders being obeyed,

> [Tu Mu says: "A general ought in time of peace to show kindly confidence in his men and also make his authority respected, so that when they come to face the enemy, orders may be executed and discipline maintained, because they all trust and look up to him." What Sun Tzŭ has said in § 44, however, would lead one rather to expect something like this: "If a general is always confident that his orders will be carried out," etc."]

the gain will be mutual.

[Chang Yu says: "The general has confidence in the men under his command, and the men are docile, having confidence in him. Thus the gain is mutual." He quotes a pregnant sentence from Wei Liao Tzŭ, ch. 4: "The art of giving orders is not to try to rectify minor blunders and not to be swayed by petty doubts." Vacillation and fussiness are the surest means of sapping the confidence of an army.]

CHAPTER 10

Terrain

[Only about a third of the chapter, comprising §§ 1-13, deals with "terrain," the subject being more fully treated in ch. XI. The "six calamities" are discussed in §§ 14-20, and the rest of the chapter is again a mere string of desultory remarks, though not less interesting, perhaps, on that account.]

1. Sun Tzŭ said: We may distinguish six kinds of terrain, to wit: (1) Accessible ground;

[Mei Yao-ch'en says: "plentifully provided with roads and means of communications."]

(2) entangling ground;

[The same commentator says: "Net-like country, venturing into which you become entangled."]

(3) temporising ground;

[Ground which allows you to "stave off" or "delay."]

(4) narrow passes; (5) precipitous heights; (6) positions at a great distance from the enemy.

[It is hardly necessary to point out the faultiness of this classification. A strange lack of logical perception is shown in the Chinaman's unquestioning acceptance of glaring cross-divisions such as the above.]

2. Ground which can be freely traversed by both sides is called *accessible.*

3. With regard to ground of this nature, be before the enemy in occupying the raised and sunny spots, and carefully guard your line of supplies.

[The general meaning of the last phrase is doubtlessly, as Tu Yu says, "not to allow the enemy to cut your communications." In view of Napoleon's dictum, "the secret of war lies in the communications,"[1] we could wish that Sun Tzŭ had done more than skirt the edge of this important subject here and in I. § 10, VII. § 11. Col. Henderson says: "The line of supply may be said to be as vital to the existence of an army as the heart to the life of a human being. Just as the duelist who finds his adversary's point menacing him with certain death, and his own guard astray, is compelled to conform to his adversary's movements, and to content himself with warding off his thrusts, so the commander whose communications are suddenly threatened finds himself in a false position, and he will be fortunate if he has not to change all his plans, to split up his force into more or less isolated detachments, and to fight with inferior numbers on ground which he has not had time to prepare, and where defeat will not be an ordinary failure, but will entail the ruin or surrender of his whole army."[2]]

Then you will be able to fight with advantage.

4. Ground which can be abandoned but is hard to re-occupy is called *entangling.*

---

1. See "Pensees de Napoleon 1er," no. 47.

2. "The Science of War," chap. 2.

5. From a position of this sort, if the enemy is unprepared, you may sally forth and defeat him. But if the enemy is prepared for your coming, and you fail to defeat him, then, return being impossible, disaster will ensue.

6. When the position is such that neither side will gain by making the first move, it is called *temporising* ground.

> [Tu Mu says: "Each side finds it inconvenient to move, and the situation remains at a deadlock."]

7. In a position of this sort, even though the enemy should offer us an attractive bait,

> [Tu Yu says, "turning their backs on us and pretending to flee." But this is only one of the lures which might induce us to quit our position.]

it will be advisable not to stir forth, but rather to retreat, thus enticing the enemy in his turn; then, when part of his army has come out, we may deliver our attack with advantage.

8. With regard to *narrow passes*, if you can occupy them first, let them be strongly garrisoned and await the advent of the enemy.

> [Because then, as Tu Yu observes, "the initiative will lie with us, and by making sudden and unexpected attacks we shall have the enemy at our mercy."]

9. Should the enemy forestall you in occupying a pass, do not go after him if the pass is fully garrisoned, but only if it is weakly garrisoned.

10. With regard to *precipitous heights*, if you are beforehand with your adversary, you should occupy the raised and sunny spots, and there wait for him to come up.

> [Ts'ao Kung says: "The particular advantage of securing heights and defiles is that your actions cannot then be dictated by the enemy." [For the enunciation of the grand principle alluded to, see VI. § 2].

Chang Yu tells the following anecdote of P'ei Hsing-chien (A.D. 619-682), who was sent on a punitive expedition against the Turkic tribes. "At night he pitched his camp as usual, and it had already been completely fortified by wall and ditch, when suddenly he gave orders that the army should shift its quarters to a hill near by. This was highly displeasing to his officers, who protested loudly against the extra fatigue which it would entail on the men. P'ei Hsing-chien, however, paid no heed to their remonstrances and had the camp moved as quickly as possible. The same night, a terrific storm came on, which flooded their former place of encampment to the depth of over twelve feet. The recalcitrant officers were amazed at the sight, and owned that they had been in the wrong. 'How did you know what was going to happen?' they asked. P'ei Hsing-chien replied: 'From this time forward be content to obey orders without asking unnecessary questions.' From this it may be seen," Chang Yu continues, "that high and sunny places are advantageous not only for fighting, but also because they are immune from disastrous floods."]

11. If the enemy has occupied them before you, do not follow him, but retreat and try to entice him away.

[The turning point of Li Shih-min's campaign in 621 A.D. against the two rebels, Tou Chien-te, King of Hsia, and Wang Shih-ch'ung, Prince of Cheng, was his seizure of the heights of Wu-lao, in spite of which Tou Chien-te persisted in his attempt to relieve his ally in Lo-yang, was defeated and taken prisoner. See *Chiu T'ang Shu*, ch. 2, fol. 5 verso, and also ch. 54.]

12. If you are situated at a great distance from the enemy, and the strength of the two armies is equal, it is not easy to provoke a battle,

[The point is that we must not think of undertaking a long and wearisome march, at the end of which, as Tu Yu says, "we should be exhausted and our adversary fresh and keen."]

and fighting will be to your disadvantage.

13. These six are the principles connected with Earth.

[Or perhaps, "the principles relating to ground." See, however, I. § 8.]

The general who has attained a responsible post must be careful to study them.

14. Now an army is exposed to six several calamities, not arising from natural causes, but from faults for which the general is responsible. These are: (1) Flight; (2) insubordination; (3) collapse; (4) ruin; (5) disorganisation; (6) rout.

15. Other conditions being equal, if one force is hurled against another ten times its size, the result will be the *flight* of the former.

16. When the common soldiers are too strong and their officers too weak, the result is *insubordination.*

[Tu Mu cites the unhappy case of T'ien Pu [*Hsin T'ang Shu*, ch. 148], who was sent to Wei in 821 A.D. with orders to lead an army against Wang T'ing-ts'ou. But the whole time he was in command, his soldiers treated him with the utmost contempt, and openly flouted his authority by riding about the camp on donkeys, several thousands at a time. T'ien Pu was powerless to put a stop to this conduct, and when, after some months had passed, he made an attempt to engage the enemy, his troops turned tail and dispersed in every direction. After that, the unfortunate man committed suicide by cutting his throat.]

When the officers are too strong and the common soldiers too weak, the result is *collapse.*

[Ts'ao Kung says: "The officers are energetic and want to press on, the common soldiers are feeble and suddenly collapse."]

17. When the higher officers are angry and insubordinate, and on meeting the enemy give battle on their own account from a feeling of resentment, before the commander-in-chief can tell whether or no he is in a position to fight, the result is *ruin.*

[Wang Hsi's note is: "This means, the general is angry without cause, and at the same time does not appreciate the ability of his subordinate officers; thus he arouses fierce resentment and brings an avalanche of ruin upon his head."]

18. When the general is weak and without authority; when his orders are not clear and distinct;

[Wei Liao Tzŭ (ch. 4) says: "If the commander gives his orders with decision, the soldiers will not wait to hear them twice; if his moves are made without vacillation, the soldiers will not be in two minds about doing their duty." General Baden-Powell says, italicizing the words: "The secret of getting successful work out of your trained men lies in one nutshell—in the clearness of the instructions they receive."[3] Cf. also Wu Tzŭ ch. 3: "the most fatal defect in a military leader is difference; the worst calamities that befall an army arise from hesitation."]

when there are no fixed duties assigned to officers and men,

[Tu Mu says: "Neither officers nor men have any regular routine."]

and the ranks are formed in a slovenly haphazard manner, the result is utter *disorganisation*.

19. When a general, unable to estimate the enemy's strength, allows an inferior force to engage a larger one, or hurls a weak detachment against a powerful one, and neglects to place picked soldiers in the front rank, the result must be a *rout*.

[Chang Yu paraphrases the latter part of the sentence and continues: "Whenever there is fighting to be done, the keenest spirits should be appointed to serve in the front ranks, both in order to strengthen the resolution of our own men and to demoralize the enemy." Cf. the primi ordines of Caesar ("De Bello Gallico," V. 28, 44, et al.).]

---

3. "Aids to Scouting," p. xii.

20. These are six ways of courting defeat, which must be carefully noted by the general who has attained a responsible post.

[See *supra*, § 13.]

21. The natural formation of the country is the soldier's best ally;

[Ch'en Hao says: "The advantages of weather and season are not equal to those connected with ground."]

but a power of estimating the adversary, of controlling the forces of victory, and of shrewdly calculating difficulties, dangers and distances, constitutes the test of a great general.

22. He who knows these things, and in fighting puts his knowledge into practice, will win his battles. He who knows them not, nor practises them, will surely be defeated.

23. If fighting is sure to result in victory, then you must fight, even though the ruler forbid it; if fighting will not result in victory, then you must not fight even at the ruler's bidding.

[Cf. VIII. § 3 fin. Huang Shih-kung of the Ch'in dynasty, who is said to have been the patron of Chang Liang and to have written the *San Lueh*, has these words attributed to him: "The responsibility of setting an army in motion must devolve on the general alone; if advance and retreat are controlled from the Palace, brilliant results will hardly be achieved. Hence the god-like ruler and the enlightened monarch are content to play a humble part in furthering their country's cause [lit., kneel down to push the chariot wheel]." This means that "in matters lying outside the zenana, the decision of the military commander must be absolute." Chang Yu also quote the saying: "Decrees from the Son of Heaven do not penetrate the walls of a camp."]

24. The general who advances without coveting fame and retreats without fearing disgrace,

[It was Wellington, I think, who said that the hardest thing of all for a soldier is to retreat.]

whose only thought is to protect his country and do good service for his sovereign, is the jewel of the kingdom.

[A noble presentiment, in few words, of the Chinese "happy warrior." Such a man, says Ho Shih, "even if he had to suffer punishment, would not regret his conduct."]

25. Regard your soldiers as your children, and they will follow you into the deepest valleys; look on them as your own beloved sons, and they will stand by you even unto death.

[Cf. I. § 6. In this connection, Tu Mu draws for us an engaging picture of the famous general Wu Ch'i, from whose treatise on war I have frequently had occasion to quote: "He wore the same clothes and ate the same food as the meanest of his soldiers, refused to have either a horse to ride or a mat to sleep on, carried his own surplus rations wrapped in a parcel, and shared every hardship with his men. One of his soldiers was suffering from an abscess, and Wu Ch'i himself sucked out the virus. The soldier's mother, hearing this, began wailing and lamenting. Somebody asked her, saying: 'Why do you cry? Your son is only a common soldier, and yet the commander-in-chief himself has sucked the poison from his sore.' The woman replied, 'Many years ago, Lord Wu performed a similar service for my husband, who never left him afterwards, and finally met his death at the hands of the enemy. And now that he has done the same for my son, he too will fall fighting I know not where.'" Li Ch'uan mentions the Viscount of Ch'u, who invaded the small state of Hsiao during the winter. The Duke of Shen said to him: "Many of the soldiers are suffering severely from the cold." So he made a round of the whole army, comforting and encouraging the men; and straightway they felt as if they were clothed in garments lined with floss silk.]

26. If, however, you are indulgent, but unable to make your authority felt; kind-hearted, but unable to enforce your commands; and incapable, moreover, of quelling disorder: then your soldiers

must be likened to spoilt children; they are useless for any practical purpose.

[Li Ching once said that if you could make your soldiers afraid of you, they would not be afraid of the enemy. Tu Mu recalls an instance of stern military discipline which occurred in 219 A.D., when Lu Meng was occupying the town of Chiang-ling. He had given stringent orders to his army not to molest the inhabitants nor take anything from them by force. Nevertheless, a certain officer serving under his banner, who happened to be a fellow-townsman, ventured to appropriate a bamboo hat belonging to one of the people, in order to wear it over his regulation helmet as a protection against the rain. Lu Meng considered that the fact of his being also a native of Ju-nan should not be allowed to palliate a clear breach of discipline, and accordingly he ordered his summary execution, the tears rolling down his face, however, as he did so. This act of severity filled the army with wholesome awe, and from that time forth even articles dropped in the highway were not picked up.]

27. If we know that our own men are in a condition to attack, but are unaware that the enemy is not open to attack, we have gone only halfway towards victory.

[That is, Ts'ao Kung says, "the issue in this case is uncertain."]

28. If we know that the enemy is open to attack, but are unaware that our own men are not in a condition to attack, we have gone only halfway towards victory.

[Cf. III. § 13 (1).]

29. If we know that the enemy is open to attack, and also know that our men are in a condition to attack, but are unaware that the nature of the ground makes fighting impracticable, we have still gone only halfway towards victory.

30. Hence the experienced soldier, once in motion, is never bewildered; once he has broken camp, he is never at a loss.

[The reason being, according to Tu Mu, that he has taken his measures so thoroughly as to ensure victory beforehand. "He does not move recklessly," says Chang Yu, "so that when he does move, he makes no mistakes."]

31. Hence the saying: If you know the enemy and know yourself, your victory will not stand in doubt; if you know Heaven and know Earth, you may make your victory complete.

[Li Ch'uan sums up as follows: "Given a knowledge of three things—the affairs of men, the seasons of heaven and the natural advantages of earth—, victory will invariably crown your battles."]

CHAPTER 11

The Nine Situations

1. Sun Tzŭ said: The art of war recognises nine varieties of ground: (1) Dispersive ground; (2) facile ground; (3) contentious ground; (4) open ground; (5) ground of intersecting highways; (6) serious ground; (7) difficult ground; (8) hemmed-in ground; (9) desperate ground.

2. When a chieftain is fighting in his own territory, it is dispersive ground.

[So called because the soldiers, being near to their homes and anxious to see their wives and children, are likely to seize the opportunity afforded by a battle and scatter in every direction. "In their advance," observes Tu Mu, "they will lack the valor of desperation, and when they retreat, they will find harbors of refuge."]

3. When he has penetrated into hostile territory, but to no great distance, it is facile ground.

[Li Ch'uan and Ho Shih say "because of the facility for retreating," and the other commentators give similar explanations. Tu Mu remarks: "When your army has crossed the border, you should burn your boats and bridges, in order to make it clear to everybody that you have no hankering after home."]

4. Ground the possession of which imports great advantage to either side, is contentious ground.

[Tu Mu defines the ground as ground "to be contended for." Ts'ao Kung says: "ground on which the few and the weak can defeat the many and the strong," such as "the neck of a pass," instanced by Li Ch'uan. Thus, Thermopylae was of this classification because the possession of it, even for a few days only, meant holding the entire invading army in check and thus gaining invaluable time. Cf. Wu Tzŭ, ch. V. ad init.: "For those who have to fight in the ratio of one to ten, there is nothing better than a narrow pass." When Lu Kuang was returning from his triumphant expedition to Turkestan in 385 A.D., and had got as far as I-ho, laden with spoils, Liang Hsi, administrator of Liang-chou, taking advantage of the death of Fu Chien, King of Ch'in, plotted against him and was for barring his way into the province. Yang Han, governor of Kao-ch'ang, counseled him, saying: "Lu Kuang is fresh from his victories in the west, and his soldiers are vigorous and mettlesome. If we oppose him in the shifting sands of the desert, we shall be no match for him, and we must therefore try a different plan. Let us hasten to occupy the defile at the mouth of the Kao-wu pass, thus cutting him off from supplies of water, and when his troops are prostrated with thirst, we can dictate our own terms without moving. Or if you think that the pass I mention is too far off, we could make a stand against him at the I-wu pass, which is nearer. The cunning and resource of Tzŭ-fang himself would be expended in vain against the enormous strength of these two positions." Liang Hsi, refusing to act on this advice, was overwhelmed and swept away by the invader.]

5. Ground on which each side has liberty of movement is open ground.

[There are various interpretations of the Chinese adjective for this type of ground. Ts'ao Kung says it means "ground covered with a network of roads," like a chessboard. Ho Shih suggested: "ground on which intercommunication is easy."]

6. Ground which forms the key to three contiguous states,

[Ts'au Kung defines this as: "Our country adjoining the enemy's and a third country conterminous with both." Meng Shih instances the small principality of Cheng, which was bounded on the north-east by Ch'i, on the west by Chin, and on the south by Ch'u.]

so that he who occupies it first has most of the Empire at his command,

[The belligerent who holds this dominating position can constrain most of them to become his allies.]

is ground of intersecting highways.

7. When an army has penetrated into the heart of a hostile country, leaving a number of fortified cities in its rear, it is serious ground.

[Wang Hsi explains the name by saying that "when an army has reached such a point, its situation is serious."]

8. Mountain forests,

[Or simply "forests."]

rugged steeps, marshes and fens—all country that is hard to traverse: this is difficult ground.

9. Ground which is reached through narrow gorges, and from which we can only retire by tortuous paths, so that a small number of the enemy would suffice to crush a large body of our men: this is hemmed in ground.

10. Ground on which we can only be saved from destruction by fighting without delay, is desperate ground.

[The situation, as pictured by Ts'ao Kung, is very similar to the "hemmed-in ground" except that here escape is no longer possible: "A lofty mountain in front, a large river behind, advance impossible, retreat blocked." Ch'en Hao says: "to be on 'desperate ground' is like sitting in a leaking boat or crouching in a burning house." Tu Mu quotes from Li Ching a vivid description of the plight of an army thus entrapped: "Suppose an army invading hostile territory without the aid of local guides:—it falls into a fatal snare and is at the enemy's mercy. A ravine on the left, a mountain on the right, a pathway so perilous that the horses have to be roped together and the chariots carried in slings, no passage open in front, retreat cut off behind, no choice but to proceed in single file. Then, before there is time to range our soldiers in order of battle, the enemy is overwhelming strength suddenly appears on the scene. Advancing, we can nowhere take a breathing-space; retreating, we have no haven of refuge. We seek a pitched battle, but in vain; yet standing on the defensive, none of us has a moment's respite. If we simply maintain our ground, whole days and months will crawl by; the moment we make a move, we have to sustain the enemy's attacks on front and rear. The country is wild, destitute of water and plants; the army is lacking in the necessaries of life, the horses are jaded and the men worn-out, all the resources of strength and skill unavailing, the pass so narrow that a single man defending it can check the onset of ten thousand; all means of offense in the hands of the enemy, all points of vantage already forfeited by ourselves:—in this terrible plight, even though we had the most valiant soldiers and the keenest of weapons, how could they be employed with the slightest effect?" Students of Greek history may be reminded of the awful close to the Sicilian expedition, and the agony of the Athenians under Nicias and Demonsthenes. [See Thucydides, VII. 78 sqq.].]

11. On dispersive ground, therefore, fight not. On facile ground, halt not. On contentious ground, attack not.

[But rather let all your energies be bent on occupying the advantageous position first. So Ts'ao Kung. Li Ch'uan and others, however, suppose the meaning to be that the enemy has already forestalled us, sot that it would be sheer madness to attack. In the *Sun Tzŭ Hsu Lu*, when the King of Wu inquires what should be done in this case, Sun Tzŭ replies: "The rule with regard to contentious ground is that those in possession have the advantage over the other side. If a position of this kind is secured first by the enemy, beware of attacking him. Lure him away by pretending to flee—show your banners and sound your drums—make a dash for other places that he cannot afford to lose—trail brushwood and raise a dust—confound his ears and eyes—detach a body of your best troops, and place it secretly in ambuscade. Then your opponent will sally forth to the rescue."]

12. On open ground, do not try to block the enemy's way.

[Because the attempt would be futile, and would expose the blocking force itself to serious risks. There are two interpretations available here. I follow that of Chang Yu. The other is indicated in Ts'ao Kung's brief note: "Draw closer together"—i.e., see that a portion of your own army is not cut off.]

On ground of intersecting highways, join hands with your allies.

[Or perhaps, "form alliances with neighbouring states."]

13. On serious ground, gather in plunder.

[On this, Li Ch'uan has the following delicious note: "When an army penetrates far into the enemy's country, care must be taken not to alienate the people by unjust treatment. Follow the example of the Han Emperor Kao Tsu, whose march into Ch'in territory was marked by no violation of women or looting of valuables. [Nota bene: this was in 207 B.C., and may well cause us to blush for the Christian armies that entered Peking in 1900 A.D.] Thus he won the hearts of all. In the present passage, then, I think that the true reading must be, not 'plunder,' but 'do not plunder.'" Alas, I fear that in this instance the worthy commentator's feelings outran his judgment. Tu Mu, at least, has no such illusions. He says: "When encamped on 'serious ground,' there being no inducement as yet to advance further, and no possibility of retreat, one ought to take measures for a protracted resistance by bringing in provisions from all sides, and keep a close watch on the enemy."]

In difficult ground, keep steadily on the march.

[Or, in the words of VIII. § 2, "do not encamp."]

14. On hemmed-in ground, resort to stratagem.

[Ts'au Kung says: "Try the effect of some unusual artifice;" and Tu Yu amplifies this by saying: "In such a position, some scheme must be devised which will suit the circumstances, and if we can succeed in deluding the enemy, the peril may be escaped." This is exactly what happened on the famous occasion when Hannibal was hemmed in among the mountains on the road to Casilinum, and to all appearances entrapped by the dictator Fabius. The stratagem which Hannibal devised to baffle his foes was remarkably like that which T'ien Tan had also employed with success exactly 62 years before. [See IX. § 24, note.] When night came on, bundles of twigs were fastened to the horns of some 2000 oxen and set on fire, the terrified animals being then quickly driven along the mountain side towards the passes which were beset by the enemy. The strange spectacle of these rapidly moving lights so alarmed and discomfited the Romans that they withdrew from their position, and Hannibal's army passed safely through the defile. [See Polybius, III. 93, 94; Livy, XXII. 16 17.]]

On desperate ground, fight.

[For, as Chia Lin remarks: "if you fight with all your might, there is a chance of life; where as death is certain if you cling to your corner."]

15. Those who were called skilful leaders of old knew how to drive a wedge between the enemy's front and rear;

[More literally, "cause the front and rear to lose touch with each other."]

to prevent co-operation between his large and small divisions; to hinder the good troops from rescuing the bad, the officers from rallying their men.

16. When the enemy's men were scattered, they prevented them from concentrating; even when their forces were united, they managed to keep them in disorder.

17. When it was to their advantage, they made a forward move; when otherwise, they stopped still.

[Mei Yao-ch'en connects this with the foregoing: "Having succeeded in thus dislocating the enemy, they would push forward in order to secure any advantage to be gained; if there was no advantage to be gained, they would remain where they were."]

18. If asked how to cope with a great host of the enemy in orderly array and on the point of marching to the attack, I should say: "Begin by seizing something which your opponent holds dear; then he will be amenable to your will."

[Opinions differ as to what Sun Tzŭ had in mind. Ts'ao Kung thinks it is "some strategical advantage on which the enemy is depending." Tu Mu says: "The three things which an enemy is anxious to do, and on the accomplishment of which his success depends, are: (1) to capture our favourable positions; (2) to ravage our cultivated land; (3) to guard his own communications." Our object then must be to thwart his plans in these three directions and thus render him helpless. [Cf. III. § 3.] By boldly seizing the initiative in this way, you at once throw the other side on the defensive.]

19. Rapidity is the essence of war:

[According to Tu Mu, "this is a summary of leading principles in warfare," and he adds: "These are the profoundest truths of military science, and the chief business of the general." The following anecdotes, told by Ho Shih, shows the importance attached to speed by two of China's greatest generals. In 227 A.D., Meng Ta, governor of Hsin-ch'eng under the Wei Emperor Wen Ti, was meditating defection to the House of Shu, and had entered into correspondence with Chu-ko Liang, Prime Minister of that State. The Wei general Ssu-ma I was then military governor of Wan, and getting wind of Meng Ta's treachery, he at once set off with an army to anticipate his revolt, having previously cajoled him by a specious message of friendly import. Ssu-ma's officers came to him and said: "If Meng Ta has leagued himself with Wu and Shu, the matter should be thoroughly investigated before we make a move." Ssu-ma I replied: "Meng Ta is an unprincipled man, and we ought to go and punish him at once, while he is still wavering and before he has thrown off the mask." Then, by a series of forced marches, be brought his army under the walls of Hsin-ch'eng with in a space of eight days. Now Meng Ta had previously said in a letter to Chu-ko Liang: "Wan is 1200 *li* from here. When the news of my revolt reaches Ssu-ma I, he will at once inform his imperial master, but it will be a whole month before any steps can be taken, and by that time my city will be well fortified. Besides, Ssu-ma I is sure not to come himself, and the generals that will be sent against us are not worth troubling about." The next letter, however, was filled with consternation: "Though only eight days have passed since I threw off my allegiance, an army is already at the city-gates. What miraculous rapidity is this!" A fortnight later, Hsin-ch'eng had fallen and Meng Ta had lost his head. [See *Chin Shu*, ch. 1, f. 3.] In 621 A.D., Li Ching was sent from K'uei-chou in Ssu-ch'uan to reduce the successful rebel Hsiao Hsien, who had set up as Emperor at the modern Ching-chou Fu in Hupeh. It was autumn, and the Yangtsze being then in flood, Hsiao Hsien never dreamt that his adversary would venture to come down through the gorges, and consequently made no preparations. But Li Ching embarked his army without loss of time, and was just about to start when the other generals implored him to postpone his departure until the river was in a less dangerous state for navigation. Li Ching replied: "To the soldier, overwhelming speed is of paramount importance, and he must never miss opportunities. Now is the time to strike, before Hsiao Hsien even knows that we have got an army together. If we seize the present moment when the river is in flood, we shall appear before his capital with startling suddenness, like the thunder which is heard before you have time to stop your ears against it. [See VII. § 19, note.] This is the great principle in war. Even if he gets to know of our approach, he will have to levy his soldiers in such a hurry that they will not be fit to oppose us. Thus the full fruits of victory will be ours." All came about as he predicted, and Hsiao Hsien was obliged to surrender, nobly stipulating that his people should be spared and he alone suffer the penalty of death.]

take advantage of the enemy's unreadiness, make your way by unexpected routes, and attack unguarded spots.

20. The following are the principles to be observed by an invading force: The further you penetrate into a country, the greater will be the solidarity of your troops, and thus the defenders will not prevail against you.

21. Make forays in fertile country in order to supply your army with food.

[Cf. *supra*, § 13. Li Ch'uan does not venture on a note here.]

22. Carefully study the well-being of your men,

[For "well-being", Wang Hsi means, "Pet them, humor them, give them plenty of food and drink, and look after them generally."]

and do not overtax them. Concentrate your energy and hoard your strength.

[Ch'en recalls the line of action adopted in 224 B.C. by the famous general Wang Chien, whose military genius largely contributed to the success of the First Emperor. He had invaded the Ch'u State, where a universal levy was made to oppose him. But, being doubtful of the temper of his troops, he declined all invitations to fight and remained strictly on the defensive. In vain did the Ch'u general try to force a battle: day after day Wang Chien kept inside his walls and would not come out, but devoted his whole time and energy to winning the affection and confidence of his men. He took care that they should be well fed, sharing his own meals with them, provided facilities for bathing, and employed every method of judicious indulgence to weld them into a loyal and homogenous body. After some time had elapsed, he told off certain persons to find out how the men were amusing themselves. The answer was, that they were contending with one another in putting the weight and long-jumping. When Wang Chien heard that they were engaged in these athletic pursuits, he knew that their spirits had been strung up to the required pitch and that they were now ready for fighting. By this time the Ch'u army, after repeating their challenge again and again, had marched away eastwards in disgust. The Ch'in general immediately broke up his camp and followed them, and in the battle that ensued they were routed with great slaughter. Shortly afterwards, the whole of Ch'u was conquered by Ch'in, and the king Fu-ch'u led into captivity.]

Keep your army continually on the move,

[In order that the enemy may never know exactly where you are. It has struck me, however, that the true reading might be "link your army together."]

and devise unfathomable plans.

23. Throw your soldiers into positions whence there is no escape, and they will prefer death to flight. If they will face death, there is nothing they may not achieve.

[Chang Yu quotes his favourite Wei Liao Tzŭ (ch. 3): "If one man were to run amok with a sword in the market-place, and everybody else tried to get our of his way, I should not allow that this man alone had courage and that all the rest were contemptible cowards. The truth is, that a desperado and a man who sets some value on his life do not meet on even terms."]

Officers and men alike will put forth their uttermost strength.

[Chang Yu says: "If they are in an awkward place together, they will surely exert their united strength to get out of it."]

24. Soldiers when in desperate straits lose the sense of fear. If there is no place of refuge, they will stand firm. If they are in the heart of a hostile country, they will show a stubborn front. If there is no help for it, they will fight hard.

25. Thus, without waiting to be marshalled, the soldiers will be constantly on the *qui vive*; without waiting to be asked, they will do your will;

[Literally, "without asking, you will get."]

without restrictions, they will be faithful; without giving orders, they can be trusted.

26. Prohibit the taking of omens, and do away with superstitious doubts. Then, until death itself comes, no calamity need be feared.

[The superstitious, "bound in to saucy doubts and fears," degenerate into cowards and "die many times before their deaths." Tu Mu quotes Huang Shih-kung: "'Spells and incantations should be strictly forbidden, and no officer allowed to inquire by divination into the fortunes of an army, for fear the soldiers' minds should be seriously perturbed.' The meaning is," he continues, "that if all doubts and scruples are discarded, your men will never falter in their resolution until they die."]

27. If our soldiers are not overburdened with money, it is not because they have a distaste for riches; if their lives are not unduly long, it is not because they are disinclined to longevity.

[Chang Yu has the best note on this passage: "Wealth and long life are things for which all men have a natural inclination. Hence, if they burn or fling away valuables, and sacrifice their own lives, it is not that they dislike them, but simply that they have no choice." Sun Tzŭ is slyly insinuating that, as soldiers are but human, it is for the general to see that temptations to shirk fighting and grow rich are not thrown in their way.]

28. On the day they are ordered out to battle, your soldiers may weep,

[The word in the Chinese is "snivel." This is taken to indicate more genuine grief than tears alone.]

those sitting up bedewing their garments, and those lying down letting the tears run down their cheeks.

[Not because they are afraid, but because, as Ts'ao Kung says, "all have embraced the firm resolution to do or die." We may remember that the heroes of the Iliad were equally childlike in showing their emotion. Chang Yu alludes to the mournful parting at the I River between Ching K'o and his friends, when the former was sent to attempt the life of the King of Ch'in (afterwards First Emperor) in 227 B.C. The tears of all flowed down like rain as he bade them farewell and uttered the following lines: "The shrill blast is blowing, Chilly the burn; Your champion is going—Not to return."[1]]

But let them once be brought to bay, and they will display the courage of a Chu or a Kuei.

[Chu was the personal name of Chuan Chu, a native of the Wu State and contemporary with Sun Tzŭ himself, who was employed by Kung-tzu Kuang, better known as Ho Lu Wang, to assassinate his sovereign Wang Liao with a dagger which he secreted in the belly of a fish served up at a banquet. He succeeded in his attempt, but was immediately hacked to pieces by the

---

1. Giles' Biographical Dictionary, no. 399.

king's bodyguard. This was in 515 B.C. The other hero referred to, Ts'ao Kuei (or Ts'ao Mo), performed the exploit which has made his name famous 166 years earlier, in 681 B.C. Lu had been thrice defeated by Ch'i, and was just about to conclude a treaty surrendering a large slice of territory, when Ts'ao Kuei suddenly seized Huan Kung, the Duke of Ch'i, as he stood on the altar steps and held a dagger against his chest. None of the duke's retainers dared to move a muscle, and Ts'ao Kuei proceeded to demand full restitution, declaring the Lu was being unjustly treated because she was a smaller and a weaker state. Huan Kung, in peril of his life, was obliged to consent, whereupon Ts'ao Kuei flung away his dagger and quietly resumed his place amid the terrified assemblage without having so much as changed color. As was to be expected, the Duke wanted afterwards to repudiate the bargain, but his wise old counselor Kuan Chung pointed out to him the impolicy of breaking his word, and the upshot was that this bold stroke regained for Lu the whole of what she had lost in three pitched battles.]

29. The skilful tactician may be likened to the shuai-jan. Now the *shuai-jan* is a snake that is found in the Ch'ang mountains.

["*Shuai-jan*" means "suddenly" or "rapidly," and the snake in question was doubtless so called owing to the rapidity of its movements. Through this passage, the term in the Chinese has now come to be used in the sense of "military manoeuvers."]

Strike at its head, and you will be attacked by its tail; strike at its tail, and you will be attacked by its head; strike at its middle, and you will be attacked by head and tail both.

30. Asked if an army can be made to imitate the *shuai-jan*,

[That is, as Mei Yao-ch'en says, "Is it possible to make the front and rear of an army each swiftly responsive to attack on the other, just as though they were part of a single living body?"]

I should answer, Yes. For the men of Wu and the men of Yüeh are enemies;

[Cf. VI. § 21.]

yet if they are crossing a river in the same boat and are caught by a storm, they will come to each other's assistance just as the left hand helps the right.

[The meaning is: If two enemies will help each other in a time of common peril, how much more should two parts of the same army, bound together as they are by every tie of interest and fellow-feeling. Yet it is notorious that many a campaign has been ruined through lack of cooperation, especially in the case of allied armies.]

31. Hence it is not enough to put one's trust in the tethering of horses, and the burying of chariot wheels in the ground.

[These quaint devices to prevent one's army from running away recall the Athenian hero Sophanes, who carried the anchor with him at the battle of Plataea, by means of which he fastened himself firmly to one spot. [See Herodotus, IX. 74.] It is not enough, says Sun Tzŭ, to render flight impossible by such mechanical means. You will not succeed unless your men have tenacity and unity of purpose, and, above all, a spirit of sympathetic cooperation. This is the lesson which can be learned from the *shuai-jan*.]

32. The principle on which to manage an army is to set up one standard of courage which all must reach.

[Literally, "level the courage [of all] as though [it were that of] one." If the ideal army is to form a single organic whole, then it follows that the resolution and spirit of its component parts must be of the same quality, or at any rate must not fall below a certain standard. Wellington's seemingly ungrateful description of his army at Waterloo as "the worst he had ever commanded" meant no more than that it was deficient in this important particular—

unity of spirit and courage. Had he not foreseen the Belgian defections and carefully kept those troops in the background, he would almost certainly have lost the day.]

33. How to make the best of both strong and weak—that is a question involving the proper use of ground.

[Mei Yao-ch'en's paraphrase is: "The way to eliminate the differences of strong and weak and to make both serviceable is to utilize accidental features of the ground." Less reliable troops, if posted in strong positions, will hold out as long as better troops on more exposed terrain. The advantage of position neutralizes the inferiority in stamina and courage. Col. Henderson says: "With all respect to the text books, and to the ordinary tactical teaching, I am inclined to think that the study of ground is often overlooked, and that by no means sufficient importance is attached to the selection of positions… and to the immense advantages that are to be derived, whether you are defending or attacking, from the proper utilization of natural features."[2]]

34. Thus the skilful general conducts his army just as though he were leading a single man, willy-nilly, by the hand.

[Tu Mu says: "The simile has reference to the ease with which he does it."]

35. It is the business of a general to be quiet and thus ensure secrecy; upright and just, and thus maintain order.

36. He must be able to mystify his officers and men by false reports and appearances,

[Literally, "to deceive their eyes and ears."]

and thus keep them in total ignorance.

[Ts'ao Kung gives us one of his excellent apophthegms: "The troops

2. "The Science of War," p. 333.

must not be allowed to share your schemes in the beginning; they may only rejoice with you over their happy outcome." "To mystify, mislead, and surprise the enemy," is one of the first principles in war, as had been frequently pointed out. But how about the other process—the mystification of one's own men? Those who may think that Sun Tzŭ is over-emphatic on this point would do well to read Col. Henderson's remarks on Stonewall Jackson's Valley campaign: "The infinite pains," he says, "with which Jackson sought to conceal, even from his most trusted staff officers, his movements, his intentions, and his thoughts, a commander less thorough would have pronounced useless"—etc. etc.[3] In the year 88 A.D., as we read in ch. 47 of the *Hou Han Shu*, "Pan Ch'ao took the field with 25,000 men from Khotan and other Central Asian states with the object of crushing Yarkand. The King of Kutcha replied by dispatching his chief commander to succour the place with an army drawn from the kingdoms of Wen-su, Ku-mo, and Wei-t'ou, totaling 50,000 men. Pan Ch'ao summoned his officers and also the King of Khotan to a council of war, and said: 'Our forces are now outnumbered and unable to make head against the enemy. The best plan, then, is for us to separate and disperse, each in a different direction. The King of Khotan will march away by the easterly route, and I will then return myself towards the west. Let us wait until the evening drum has sounded and then start.' Pan Ch'ao now secretly released the prisoners whom he had taken alive, and the King of Kutcha was thus informed of his plans. Much elated by the news, the latter set off at once at the head of 10,000 horsemen to bar Pan Ch'ao's retreat in the west, while the King of Wen-su rode eastward with 8000 horse in order to intercept the King of Khotan. As soon as Pan Ch'ao knew that the two chieftains had gone, he called his divisions together, got them well in hand, and at cock-crow hurled them against the army of Yarkand, as it lay encamped. The barbarians, panic-stricken, fled

3. "Stonewall Jackson," vol. I, p. 421.

in confusion, and were closely pursued by Pan Ch'ao. Over 5000 heads were brought back as trophies, besides immense spoils in the shape of horses and cattle and valuables of every description. Yarkand then capitulating, Kutcha and the other kingdoms drew off their respective forces. From that time forward, Pan Ch'ao's prestige completely overawed the countries of the west." In this case, we see that the Chinese general not only kept his own officers in ignorance of his real plans, but actually took the bold step of dividing his army in order to deceive the enemy.]

37. By altering his arrangements and changing his plans,

[Wang Hsi thinks that this means not using the same stratagem twice.]

he keeps the enemy without definite knowledge.

[Chang Yu, in a quotation from another work, says: "The axiom, that war is based on deception, does not apply only to deception of the enemy. You must deceive even your own soldiers. Make them follow you, but without letting them know why."]

By shifting his camp and taking circuitous routes, he prevents the enemy from anticipating his purpose.

38. At the critical moment, the leader of an army acts like one who has climbed up a height and then kicks away the ladder behind him. He carries his men deep into hostile territory before he shows his hand.

[Literally, "releases the spring" (see V. § 15), that is, takes some decisive step which makes it impossible for the army to return—like Hsiang Yu, who sunk his ships after crossing a river. Ch'en Hao, followed by Chia Lin, understands the words less well as "puts forth every artifice at his command."]

39. He burns his boats and breaks his cooking-pots; like a shepherd driving a flock of sheep, he drives his men this way and that, and none knows whither he is going.

[Tu Mu says: "The army is only cognizant of orders to advance or retreat; it is ignorant of the ulterior ends of attacking and conquering."]

40. To muster his host and bring it into danger:—this may be termed the business of the general.

[Sun Tzŭ means that after mobilization there should be no delay in aiming a blow at the enemy's heart. Note how he returns again and again to this point. Among the warring states of ancient China, desertion was no doubt a much more present fear and serious evil than it is in the armies of today.]

41. The different measures suited to the nine varieties of ground;

[Chang Yu says: "One must not be hide-bound in interpreting the rules for the nine varieties of ground."]

the expediency of aggressive or defensive tactics; and the fundamental laws of human nature: these are things that must most certainly be studied.

42. When invading hostile territory, the general principle is, that penetrating deeply brings cohesion; penetrating but a short way means dispersion.

[Cf. *supra*, § 20.]

43. When you leave your own country behind, and take your army across neighbourhood territory, you find yourself on critical ground.

[This "ground" is curiously mentioned in VIII. § 2, but it does not figure among the Nine Situations or the Six Calamities in chap. X. One's first impulse would be to translate it distant ground," but this, if we can trust the commentators, is precisely what is not meant here. Mei Yao-ch'en says it is "a position not far enough advanced to be called 'facile,' and not near enough to home to be 'dispersive,' but something between the two." Wang Hsi says: "It is ground separated from home by an interjacent state, whose territory we have had to cross in order to reach it. Hence, it is incumbent on us to settle our business there quickly." He adds that this position is of rare occurrence, which is the reason why it is not included among the Nine Situations.]

When there are means of communication on all four sides, the ground is one of intersecting highways.

44. When you penetrate deeply into a country, it is serious ground. When you penetrate but a little way, it is facile ground.

45. When you have the enemy's strongholds on your rear, and narrow passes in front, it is hemmed-in ground. When there is no place of refuge at all, it is desperate ground.

46. Therefore, on dispersive ground, I would inspire my men with unity of purpose.

[This end, according to Tu Mu, is best attained by remaining on the defensive, and avoiding battle. Cf. *supra*, § 11.]

On facile ground, I would see that there is close connection between all parts of my army.

[As Tu Mu says, the object is to guard against two possible contingencies: "(1) the desertion of our own troops; (2) a sudden attack on the part of the enemy." Cf. VII. § 17. Mei Yao-ch'en says: "On the march, the regiments should be in close touch; in an encampment, there should be continuity between the fortifications."]

47. On contentious ground, I would hurry up my rear.

[This is Ts'ao Kung's interpretation. Chang Yu adopts it, saying: "We must quickly bring up our rear, so that head and tail may both reach the goal." That is, they must not be allowed to straggle up a long way apart. Mei Yao-ch'en offers another equally plausible explanation: "Supposing the enemy has not yet reached the coveted position, and we are behind him, we should advance with all speed in order to dispute its possession." Ch'en Hao, on the other hand, assuming that the enemy has had time to select his own ground, quotes VI. § 1, where Sun Tzŭ warns us against coming exhausted to the attack. His own idea of the situation is rather vaguely expressed: "If there is a favourable position lying in front of you, detach a picked body of troops to occupy it, then if the enemy, relying on their numbers, come up to make a fight for it, you may fall quickly on their rear with your main body, and victory will be assured." It was thus, he adds, that Chao She beat the army of Ch'in. (See p. 57.)]

48. On open ground, I would keep a vigilant eye on my defences. On ground of intersecting highways, I would consolidate my alliances.

49. On serious ground, I would try to ensure a continuous stream of supplies.

[The commentators take this as referring to forage and plunder, not, as one might expect, to an unbroken communication with a home base.]

On difficult ground, I would keep pushing on along the road.

50. On hemmed-in ground, I would block any way of retreat.

[Meng Shih says: "To make it seem that I meant to defend the position, whereas my real intention is to burst suddenly through the enemy's lines." Mei Yao-ch'en says: "in order to make my soldiers fight with desperation." Wang Hsi says, "fearing lest my men be tempted to run away." Tu Mu points out that this is the converse of VII. § 36, where it is the enemy who is surrounded. In 532 A.D., Kao Huan, afterwards Emperor and canonized as Shen-wu, was surrounded by a great army under Erh-chu Chao and others. His own force was comparatively small, consisting only of 2000 horse and something under 30,000 foot. The lines of investment had not been drawn very closely together, gaps being left at certain points. But Kao Huan, instead of trying to escape, actually made a shift to block all the remaining outlets himself by driving into them a number of oxen and donkeys roped together.

As soon as his officers and men saw that there was nothing for it but to conquer or die, their spirits rose to an extraordinary pitch of exaltation, and they charged with such desperate ferocity that the opposing ranks broke and crumbled under their onslaught.]

On desperate ground, I would proclaim to my soldiers the hopelessness of saving their lives.

[Tu Yu says: "Burn your baggage and impedimenta, throw away your stores and provisions, choke up the wells, destroy your cooking-stoves, and make it plain to your men that they cannot survive, but must fight to the death." Mei Yao-ch'en says: "The only chance of life lies in giving up all hope of it." This concludes what Sun Tzŭ has to say about "grounds" and the "variations" corresponding to them. Reviewing the passages which bear on this important subject, we cannot fail to be struck by the desultory and unmethodical fashion in which it is treated. Sun Tzŭ begins abruptly in VIII. § 2 to enumerate "variations" before touching on "grounds" at all, but only mentions five, namely nos. 7, 5, 8 and 9 of the subsequent list, and one that is not included in it. A few varieties of ground are dealt with in the earlier portion of chap. IX, and then chap. X sets forth six new grounds, with six variations of plan to match. None of these is mentioned again, though the first is hardly to be distinguished from ground no. 4 in the next chapter. At last, in chap. XI, we come to the Nine Grounds par excellence, immediately followed by the variations. This takes us down to § 14. In §§ 43-45, fresh definitions are provided for nos. 5, 6, 2, 8 and 9 (in the order given), as well as for the tenth ground noticed in chap. VIII; and finally, the nine variations are enumerated once more from beginning to end, all, with the exception of 5, 6 and 7, being different from those previously given. Though it is impossible to account for the present state of Sun Tzŭ's text, a few suggestive facts maybe brought into prominence: (1) Chap. VIII, according to the title, should deal with nine variations, whereas only five appear. (2) It is an abnormally short chapter. (3) Chap. XI is entitled The Nine

Grounds. Several of these are defined twice over, besides which there are two distinct lists of the corresponding variations. (4) The length of the chapter is disproportionate, being double that of any other except IX. I do not propose to draw any inferences from these facts, beyond the general conclusion that Sun Tzŭ's work cannot have come down to us in the shape in which it left his hands: chap. VIII is obviously defective and probably out of place, while XI seems to contain matter that has either been added by a later hand or ought to appear elsewhere.]

51. For it is the soldier's disposition to offer an obstinate resistance when surrounded, to fight hard when he cannot help himself, and to obey promptly when he has fallen into danger.

[Chang Yu alludes to the conduct of Pan Ch'ao's devoted followers in 73 A.D. The story runs thus in the *Hou Han Shu*, ch. 47: "When Pan Ch'ao arrived at Shan-shan, Kuang, the King of the country, received him at first with great politeness and respect; but shortly afterwards his behavior underwent a sudden change, and he became remiss and negligent. Pan Ch'ao spoke about this to the officers of his suite: 'Have you noticed,' he said, 'that Kuang's polite intentions are on the wane? This must signify that envoys have come from the Northern barbarians, and that consequently he is in a state of indecision, not knowing with which side to throw in his lot. That surely is the reason. The truly wise man, we are told, can perceive things before they have come to pass; how much more, then, those that are already manifest!' Thereupon he called one of the natives who had been assigned to his service, and set a trap for him, saying: 'Where are those envoys from the Hsiung-nu who arrived some day ago?' The man was so taken aback that between surprise and fear he presently blurted out the whole truth. Pan Ch'ao, keeping his informant carefully under lock and key, then summoned a general gathering of his officers, thirty-six in all, and began drinking with them. When the wine had mounted into their heads a little, he tried to rouse their spirit still further by addressing them thus: 'Gentlemen, here we are in the heart of an isolated region, anxious to achieve riches and honour by some great exploit. Now it happens that an ambassador from the Hsiung-no arrived in this kingdom only a few days ago, and the result is that the respectful courtesy extended towards us by our royal host has disappeared. Should this envoy prevail upon him to seize our party and hand us over to the Hsiung-no, our bones will become food for the wolves of the desert. What are we to do?' With one accord, the officers replied: 'Standing as we do in peril of our lives, we will follow our commander through life and death.' For the sequel of this adventure, see chap. XII. § 1, note."]

52. We cannot enter into alliance with neighbouring princes until we are acquainted with their designs. We are not fit to lead an army on the march unless we are familiar with the face of the country—its mountains and forests, its pitfalls and precipices, its marshes and swamps. We shall be unable to turn natural advantages to account unless we make use of local guides.

[These three sentences are repeated from VII. §§ 12-14—in order to emphasize their importance, the commentators seem to think. I prefer to regard them as interpolated here in order to form an antecedent to the following words. With regard to local guides, Sun Tzŭ might have added that there is always the risk of going wrong, either through their treachery or some misunderstanding such as Livy records (XXII. 13): Hannibal, we are told, ordered a guide to lead him into the neighbourhood of Casinum, where there was an important pass to be occupied; but his Carthaginian accent, unsuited to the pronunciation of Latin names, caused the guide to understand Casilinum instead of Casinum, and turning from his proper route, he took the army in that direction, the mistake not being discovered until they had almost arrived.]

53. To be ignorant of any one of the following four or five principles does not befit a warlike prince.

54. When a warlike prince attacks a powerful state, his generalship shows itself in preventing the concentration of the enemy's forces. He overawes his opponents, and their allies are prevented from joining against him.

> [Mei Tao-ch'en constructs one of the chains of reasoning that are so much affected by the Chinese: "In attacking a powerful state, if you can divide her forces, you will have a superiority in strength; if you have a superiority in strength, you will overawe the enemy; if you overawe the enemy, the neighbouring states will be frightened; and if the neighbouring states are frightened, the enemy's allies will be prevented from joining her." The following gives a stronger meaning: "If the great state has once been defeated (before she has had time to summon her allies), then the lesser states will hold aloof and refrain from massing their forces." Ch'en Hao and Chang Yu take the sentence in quite another way. The former says: "Powerful though a prince may be, if he attacks a large state, he will be unable to raise enough troops, and must rely to some extent on external aid; if he dispenses with this, and with overweening confidence in his own strength, simply tries to intimidate the enemy, he will surely be defeated." Chang Yu puts his view thus: "If we recklessly attack a large state, our own people will be discontented and hang back. But if (as will then be the case) our display of military force is inferior by half to that of the enemy, the other chieftains will take fright and refuse to join us."]

55. Hence he does not strive to ally himself with all and sundry, nor does he foster the power of other states. He carries out his own secret designs, keeping his antagonists in awe.

> [The train of thought, as said by Li Ch'uan, appears to be this: Secure against a combination of his enemies, "he can afford to reject entangling alliances and simply pursue his own secret designs, his prestige enable him to dispense with external friendships."]

Thus he is able to capture their cities and overthrow their kingdoms.

[This paragraph, though written many years before the Ch'in State became a serious menace, is not a bad summary of the policy by which the famous Six Chancellors gradually paved the way for her final triumph under Shih Huang Ti. Chang Yu, following up his previous note, thinks that Sun Tzŭ is condemning this attitude of cold-blooded selfishness and haughty isolation.]

56. Bestow rewards without regard to rule,

[Wu Tzŭ (ch. 3) less wisely says: "Let advance be richly rewarded and retreat be heavily punished."]

issue orders

[Literally, "hang" or post up."]

without regard to previous arrangements;

["In order to prevent treachery," says Wang Hsi. The general meaning is made clear by Ts'ao Kung's quotation from the *Ssu-ma Fa:* "Give instructions only on sighting the enemy; give rewards when you see deserving deeds." Ts'ao Kung's paraphrase: "The final instructions you give to your army should not correspond with those that have been previously posted up." Chang Yu simplifies this into "your arrangements should not be divulged beforehand." And Chia Lin says: "there should be no fixity in your rules and arrangements." Not only is there danger in letting your plans be known, but war often necessitates the entire reversal of them at the last moment.]

and you will be able to handle a whole army as though you had to do with but a single man.

[Cf. *supra*, § 34.]

57. Confront your soldiers with the deed itself; never let them know your design.

[Literally, "do not tell them words;" i.e. do not give your reasons for any order. Lord Mansfield once told a junior colleague to "give no reasons" for his decisions, and the maxim is even more applicable to a general than to a judge.]

When the outlook is bright, bring it before their eyes; but tell them nothing when the situation is gloomy.

58. Place your army in deadly peril, and it will survive; plunge it into desperate straits, and it will come off in safety.

[These words of Sun Tzŭ were once quoted by Han Hsin in explanation of the tactics he employed in one of his most brilliant battles, already alluded to on p. 28. In 204 B.C., he was sent against the army of Chao, and halted ten miles from the mouth of the Ching-hsing pass, where the enemy had mustered in full force. Here, at midnight, he detached a body of 2000 light cavalry, every man of which was furnished with a red flag. Their instructions were to make their way through narrow defiles and keep a secret watch on the enemy. "When the men of Chao see me in full flight," Han Hsin said, "they will abandon their fortifications and give chase. This must be the sign for you to rush in, pluck down the Chao standards and set up the red banners of Han in their stead." Turning then to his other officers, he remarked: "Our adversary holds a strong position, and is not likely to come out and attack us until he sees the standard and drums of the commander-in-chief, for fear I should turn back and escape through the mountains." So saying, he first of all sent out a division consisting of 10,000 men, and ordered them to form in line of battle with their backs to the River Ti. Seeing this manoeuver, the whole army of Chao broke into loud laughter. By this time it was broad daylight, and Han Hsin, displaying the generalissimo's flag, marched out of the pass with drums beating, and was immediately engaged by the enemy. A great battle followed, lasting for some time; until at length Han Hsin and his colleague Chang Ni, leaving drums and banner on the field, fled to the division on the river bank, where another fierce battle was raging. The enemy rushed out to pursue them and to secure the trophies, thus denuding their ramparts of men;

but the two generals succeeded in joining the other army, which was fighting with the utmost desperation. The time had now come for the 2000 horsemen to play their part. As soon as they saw the men of Chao following up their advantage, they galloped behind the deserted walls, tore up the enemy's flags and replaced them by those of Han. When the Chao army looked back from the pursuit, the sight of these red flags struck them with terror. Convinced that the Hans had got in and overpowered their king, they broke up in wild disorder, every effort of their leader to stay the panic being in vain. Then the Han army fell on them from both sides and completed the rout, killing a number and capturing the rest, amongst whom was King Ya himself.... After the battle, some of Han Hsin's officers came to him and said: "In the *Art of War* we are told to have a hill or tumulus on the right rear, and a river or marsh on the left front. [This appears to be a blend of Sun Tzŭ and T'ai Kung. See IX § 9, and note.] You, on the contrary, ordered us to draw up our troops with the river at our back. Under these conditions, how did you manage to gain the victory?" The general replied: "I fear you gentlemen have not studied the Art of War with sufficient care. Is it not written there: 'Plunge your army into desperate straits and it will come off in safety; place it in deadly peril and it will survive'? Had I taken the usual course, I should never have been able to bring my colleague round. What says the Military Classic—'Swoop down on the market-place and drive the men off to fight.' [This passage does not occur in the present text of Sun Tzŭ.] If I had not placed my troops in a position where they were obliged to fight for their lives, but had allowed each man to follow his own discretion, there would have been a general *débandade*, and it would have been impossible to do anything with them." The officers admitted the force of his argument, and said: "These are higher tactics than we should have been capable of." [See *Ch'ien Han Shu*, ch. 34, ff. 4, 5.]]

59. For it is precisely when a force has fallen into harm's way that is capable of striking a blow for victory.

[Danger has a bracing effect.]

60. Success in warfare is gained by carefully accommodating ourselves to the enemy's purpose.

[Ts'ao Kung says: "Feign stupidity"—by an appearance of yielding and falling in with the enemy's wishes. Chang Yu's note makes the meaning clear: "If the enemy shows an inclination to advance, lure him on to do so; if he is anxious to retreat, delay on purpose that he may carry out his intention." The object is to make him remiss and contemptuous before we deliver our attack.]

61. By persistently hanging on the enemy's flank,

[I understand the first four words to mean "accompanying the enemy in one direction." Ts'ao Kung says: "unite the soldiers and make for the enemy." But such a violent displacement of characters is quite indefensible.]

we shall succeed in the long run

[Literally, "after a thousand *li*."]

in killing the commander-in-chief.

[Always a great point with the Chinese.]

62. This is called ability to accomplish a thing by sheer cunning.

63. On the day that you take up your command, block the frontier passes, destroy the official tallies,

[These were tablets of bamboo or wood, one half of which was issued as a permit or passport by the official in charge of a gate. Cf. the "border-warden" of *Lun Yu* III. 24, who may have had similar duties. When this half was returned to him, within a fixed period, he was authorized to open the gate and let the traveler through.]

and stop the passage of all emissaries.

[Either to or from the enemy's country.]

64. Be stern in the council-chamber,

[Show no weakness, and insist on your plans being ratified by the sovereign.]

so that you may control the situation.

[Mei Yao-ch'en understands the whole sentence to mean: Take the strictest precautions to ensure secrecy in your deliberations.]

65. If the enemy leaves a door open, you must rush in.

66. Forestall your opponent by seizing what he holds dear,

[Cf. *supra*, § 18.]

and subtly contrive to time his arrival on the ground.

[Ch'en Hao's explanation: "If I manage to seize a favourable position, but the enemy does not appear on the scene, the advantage thus obtained cannot be turned to any practical account. He who intends therefore, to occupy a position of importance to the enemy, must begin by making an artful appointment, so to speak, with his antagonist, and cajole him into going there as well." Mei Yao-ch'en explains that this "artful appointment" is to be made through the medium of the enemy's own spies, who will carry back just the amount of information that we choose to give them. Then, having cunningly disclosed our intentions, "we must manage, though starting after the enemy, to arrive before him (VII. § 4)." We must start after him in order to ensure his marching thither; we must arrive before him in order to capture the place without trouble. Taken thus, the present passage lends some support to Mei Yao-ch'en's interpretation of § 47.]

67. Walk in the path defined by rule,

[Chia Lin says: "Victory is the only thing that matters, and this cannot be achieved by adhering to conventional canons." It is unfortunate that this variant rests on very slight authority, for the sense yielded is certainly much more satisfactory. Napoleon, as we know, according to the veterans of the old school whom he defeated, won his battles by violating every accepted canon of warfare.]

and accommodate yourself to the enemy until you can fight a decisive battle.

[Tu Mu says: "Conform to the enemy's tactics until a favourable opportunity offers; then come forth and engage in a battle that shall prove decisive."]

68. At first, then, exhibit the coyness of a maiden, until the enemy gives you an opening; afterwards emulate the rapidity of a running hare, and it will be too late for the enemy to oppose you.

[As the hare is noted for its extreme timidity, the comparison hardly appears felicitous. But of course Sun Tzŭ was thinking only of its speed. The words have been taken to mean: You must flee from the enemy as quickly as an escaping hare; but this is rightly rejected by Tu Mu.]

CHAPTER 12

The Attack by Fire

[Rather more than half the chapter (§§ 1-13) is devoted to the subject of fire, after which the author branches off into other topics.]

1. Sun Tzŭ said: There are five ways of attacking with fire. The first is to burn soldiers in their camp;

[So Tu Mu. Li Ch'uan says: "Set fire to the camp, and kill the soldiers" (when they try to escape from the flames). Pan Ch'ao, sent on a diplomatic mission to the King of Shan-shan [see XI. § 51, note], found himself placed in extreme peril by the unexpected arrival of an envoy from the Hsiung-nu [the mortal enemies of the Chinese]. In consultation with his officers, he exclaimed: "'Never venture, never win![1] The only course open to us now is to make an assault by fire on the barbarians under cover of night, when they will not be able to discern our numbers. Profiting by their panic, we shall exterminate them completely; this will cool the King's courage and cover us with glory, besides ensuring the success of our mission.' The officers all replied that it would be necessary to discuss the matter first with

1. "Unless you enter the tiger's lair, you cannot get hold of the tiger's cubs."

the Intendant. Pan Ch'ao then fell into a passion: 'It is today,' he cried, 'that our fortunes must be decided! The Intendant is only a humdrum civilian, who on hearing of our project will certainly be afraid, and everything will be brought to light. An inglorious death is no worthy fate for valiant warriors.' All then agreed to do as he wished. Accordingly, as soon as night came on, he and his little band quickly made their way to the barbarian camp. A strong gale was blowing at the time. Pan Ch'ao ordered ten of the party to take drums and hide behind the enemy's barracks, it being arranged that when they saw flames shoot up, they should begin drumming and yelling with all their might. The rest of his men, armed with bows and crossbows, he posted in ambuscade at the gate of the camp. He then set fire to the place from the windward side, whereupon a deafening noise of drums and shouting arose on the front and rear of the Hsiung-nu, who rushed out pell-mell in frantic disorder. Pan Ch'ao slew three of them with his own hand, while his companions cut off the heads of the envoy and thirty of his suite. The remainder, more than a hundred in all, perished in the flames. On the following day, Pan Ch'ao, divining his thoughts, said with uplifted hand: 'Although you did not go with us last night, I should not think, Sir, of taking sole credit for our exploit.' This satisfied Kuo Hsun, and Pan Ch'ao, having sent for Kuang, King of Shan-shan, showed him the head of the barbarian envoy. The whole kingdom was seized with fear and trembling, which Pan Ch'ao took steps to allay by issuing a public proclamation. Then, taking the king's sons as hostage, he returned to make his report to Tou Ku." [*Hou Han Shu*, ch. 47, ff. 1, 2.]]

the second is to burn stores;

[Tu Mu says: "Provisions, fuel and fodder." In order to subdue the rebellious population of Kiangnan, Kao Keng recommended Wen Ti of the Sui dynasty to make periodical raids and burn their stores of grain, a policy which in the long run proved entirely successful.]

the third is to burn baggage-trains;

[An example given is the destruction of Yuan Shao's wagons and impedimenta by Ts'ao Ts'ao in 200 A.D.]

the fourth is to burn arsenals and magazines;

[Tu Mu says that the things contained in "arsenals" and "magazines" are the same. He specifies weapons and other implements, bullion and clothing. Cf. VII. § 11.]

the fifth is to hurl dropping fire amongst the enemy.

[Tu Yu says in the *T'ung Tien:* "To drop fire into the enemy's camp. The method by which this may be done is to set the tips of arrows alight by dipping them into a brazier, and then shoot them from powerful crossbows into the enemy's lines."]

2. In order to carry out an attack, we must have means available.

[T'sao Kung thinks that "traitors in the enemy's camp" are referred to. But Ch'en Hao is more likely to be right in saying: "We must have favourable circumstances in general, not merely traitors to help us." Chia Lin says: "We must avail ourselves of wind and dry weather."]

the material for raising fire should always be kept in readiness.

[Tu Mu suggests as material for making fire: "dry vegetable matter, reeds, brushwood, straw, grease, oil, etc." Here we have the material cause. Chang Yu says: "vessels for hoarding fire, stuff for lighting fires."]

3. There is a proper season for making attacks with fire, and special days for starting a conflagration.

4. The proper season is when the weather is very dry; the special days are those when the moon is in the constellations of the Sieve, the Wall, the Wing or the Cross-bar;

[These are, respectively, the 7th, 14th, 27th, and 28th of the Twenty-eight Stellar Mansions, corresponding roughly to Sagittarius, Pegasus, Crater and Corvus.]

for these four are all days of rising wind.

5. In attacking with fire, one should be prepared to meet five possible developments:

6. (1) When fire breaks out inside the enemy's camp, respond at once with an attack from without.

7. (2) If there is an outbreak of fire, but the enemy's soldiers remain quiet, bide your time and do not attack.

> [The prime object of attacking with fire is to throw the enemy into confusion. If this effect is not produced, it means that the enemy is ready to receive us. Hence the necessity for caution.]

8. (3) When the force of the flames has reached its height, follow it up with an attack, if that is practicable; if not, stay where you are.

> [Ts'ao Kung says: "If you see a possible way, advance; but if you find the difficulties too great, retire."]

9. (4) If it is possible to make an assault with fire from without, do not wait for it to break out within, but deliver your attack at a favourable moment.

> [Tu Mu says that the previous paragraphs had reference to the fire breaking out (either accidentally, we may suppose, or by the agency of incendiaries) inside the enemy's camp. "But," he continues, "if the enemy is settled in a waste place littered with quantities of grass, or if he has pitched his camp in a position which can be burnt out, we must carry our fire against him at any seasonable opportunity, and not await on in hopes of an outbreak occurring within, for fear our opponents should themselves burn up the surrounding vegetation, and thus render our own attempts fruitless." The famous Li Ling once baffled the leader of the Hsiung-nu in this way. The latter, taking advantage of a favourable wind, tried to set fire to the Chinese general's camp, but found that every scrap of combustible vegetation in the neighbourhood had already been burnt down. On the other hand, Po-ts'ai, a general of

the Yellow Turban rebels, was badly defeated in 184 A.D. through his neglect of this simple precaution. "At the head of a large army he was besieging Ch'ang-she, which was held by Huang-fu Sung. The garrison was very small, and a general feeling of nervousness pervaded the ranks; so Huang-fu Sung called his officers together and said: 'In war, there are various indirect methods of attack, and numbers do not count for everything. The commentator here quotes Sun Tzŭ, V. §§ 5, 6 and 10.] Now the rebels have pitched their camp in the midst of thick grass which will easily burn when the wind blows. If we set fire to it at night, they will be thrown into a panic, and we can make a sortie and attack them on all sides at once, thus emulating the achievement of T'ien Tan.' [See p. 90.] That same evening, a strong breeze sprang up; so Huang-fu Sung instructed his soldiers to bind reeds together into torches and mount guard on the city walls, after which he sent out a band of daring men, who stealthily made their way through the lines and started the fire with loud shouts and yells. Simultaneously, a glare of light shot up from the city walls, and Huang-fu Sung, sounding his drums, led a rapid charge, which threw the rebels into confusion and put them to headlong flight." [*Hou Han Shu*, ch. 71.]]

10. (5) When you start a fire, be to windward of it. Do not attack from the leeward.

[Chang Yu, following Tu Yu, says: "When you make a fire, the enemy will retreat away from it; if you oppose his retreat and attack him then, he will fight desperately, which will not conduce to your success." A rather more obvious explanation is given by Tu Mu: "If the wind is in the east, begin burning to the east of the enemy, and follow up the attack yourself from that side. If you start the fire on the east side, and then attack from the west, you will suffer in the same way as your enemy."]

11. A wind that rises in the daytime lasts long, but a night breeze soon falls.

[Cf. Lao Tzŭ's saying: "A violent wind does not last the space of a morning." (*Tao Te Ching*, chap. 23.) Mei Yao-ch'en and Wang Hsi say: "A day breeze dies down at nightfall, and a night breeze at daybreak. This is what happens as a general rule." The phenomenon observed may be correct enough, but how this sense is to be obtained is not apparent.]

12. In every army, the five developments connected with fire must be known, the movements of the stars calculated, and a watch kept for the proper days.

[Tu Mu says: "We must make calculations as to the paths of the stars, and watch for the days on which wind will rise, before making our attack with fire." Chang Yu seems to interpret the text differently: "We must not only know how to assail our opponents with fire, but also be on our guard against similar attacks from them."]

13. Hence those who use fire as an aid to the attack show intelligence; those who use water as an aid to the attack gain an accession of strength.

14. By means of water, an enemy may be intercepted, but not robbed of all his belongings.

[Ts'ao Kung's note is: "We can merely obstruct the enemy's road or divide his army, but not sweep away all his accumulated stores." Water can do useful service, but it lacks the terrible destructive power of fire. This is the reason, Chang Yu concludes, why the former is dismissed in a couple of sentences, whereas the attack by fire is discussed in detail. Wu Tzŭ (ch. 4) speaks thus of the two elements: "If an army is encamped on low-lying marshy ground, from which the water cannot run off, and where the rainfall is heavy, it may be submerged by a flood. If an army is encamped in wild marsh lands thickly overgrown with weeds and brambles, and visited by frequent gales, it may be exterminated by fire."]

15. Unhappy is the fate of one who tries to win his battles and succeed in his attacks without cultivating the spirit of enterprise; for the result is waste of time and general stagnation.

[This is one of the most perplexing passages in Sun Tzŭ. Ts'ao Kung says: "Rewards for good service should not be deferred a single day." And Tu Mu: "If you do not take opportunity to advance and reward the deserving, your subordinates will not carry out your commands, and disaster will ensue." For several reasons, however, and in spite of the formidable array of scholars on the other side, I prefer the interpretation suggested by Mei Yao-ch'en alone, whose words I will quote: "Those who want to make sure of succeeding in their battles and assaults must seize the favourable moments when they come and not shrink on occasion from heroic measures: that is to say, they must resort to such means of attack of fire, water and the like. What they must not do, and what will prove fatal, is to sit still and simply hold to the advantages they have got."]

16. Hence the saying: The enlightened ruler lays his plans well ahead; the good general cultivates his resources.

[Tu Mu quotes the following from the *San Lueh*, ch. 2: "The warlike prince controls his soldiers by his authority, kits them together by good faith, and by rewards makes them serviceable. If faith decays, there will be disruption; if rewards are deficient, commands will not be respected."]

17. Move not unless you see an advantage; use not your troops unless there is something to be gained; fight not unless the position is critical.

[Sun Tzŭ may at times appear to be over-cautious, but he never goes so far in that direction as the remarkable passage in the *Tao Te Ching*, ch. 69. "I dare not take the initiative, but prefer to act on the defensive; I dare not advance an inch, but prefer to retreat a foot."]

18. No ruler should put troops into the field merely to gratify his own spleen; no general should fight a battle simply out of pique.

19. If it is to your advantage, make a forward move; if not, stay where you are.

> [This is repeated from XI. § 17. Here I feel convinced that it is an interpolation, for it is evident that § 20 ought to follow immediately on § 18.]

20. Anger may in time change to gladness; vexation may be succeeded by content.

21. But a kingdom that has once been destroyed can never come again into being;

> [The Wu State was destined to be a melancholy example of this saying.]

nor can the dead ever be brought back to life.

22. Hence the enlightened ruler is heedful, and the good general full of caution. This is the way to keep a country at peace and an army intact.

CHAPTER 13

The Use of Spies

1. Sun Tzŭ said: Raising a host of a hundred thousand men and marching them great distances entails heavy loss on the people and a drain on the resources of the State. The daily expenditure will amount to a thousand ounces of silver.

[Cf. II. §§ 1, 13, 14.]

There will be commotion at home and abroad, and men will drop down exhausted on the highways.

[Cf. *Tao Te Ching*, ch. 30: "Where troops have been quartered, brambles and thorns spring up." Chang Yu has the note: "We may be reminded of the saying: 'On serious ground, gather in plunder.' Why then should carriage and transportation cause exhaustion on the highways?—The answer is, that not victuals alone, but all sorts of munitions of war have to be conveyed to the army. Besides, the injunction to 'forage on the enemy' only means that when an army is deeply engaged in hostile territory, scarcity of food must be provided against. Hence, without being solely dependent on the enemy for corn, we must forage in order that there may be an uninterrupted flow of supplies. Then, again, there are places like salt deserts where provisions being unobtainable, supplies from home cannot be dispensed with."]

As many as seven hundred thousand families will be impeded in their labor.

[Mei Yao-ch'en says: "Men will be lacking at the plough-tail." The allusion is to the system of dividing land into nine parts, each consisting of about 15 acres, the plot in the center being cultivated on behalf of the State by the tenants of the other eight. It was here also, so Tu Mu tells us, that their cottages were built and a well sunk, to be used by all in common. [See II. § 12, note.] In time of war, one of the families had to serve in the army, while the other seven contributed to its support. Thus, by a levy of 100,000 men (reckoning one able-bodied soldier to each family) the husbandry of 700,000 families would be affected.]

2. Hostile armies may face each other for years, striving for the victory which is decided in a single day. This being so, to remain in ignorance of the enemy's condition simply because one grudges the outlay of a hundred ounces of silver in honours and emoluments,

["For spies" is of course the meaning, though it would spoil the effect of this curiously elaborate exordium if spies were actually mentioned at this point.]

is the height of inhumanity.

[Sun Tzŭ's agreement is certainly ingenious. He begins by adverting to the frightful misery and vast expenditure of blood and treasure which war always brings in its train. Now, unless you are kept informed of the enemy's condition, and are ready to strike at the right moment, a war may drag on for years. The only way to get this information is to employ spies, and it is impossible to obtain trustworthy spies unless they are properly paid for their services. But it is surely false economy to grudge a comparatively trifling amount for this purpose, when every day that the war lasts eats up an incalculably greater sum. This grievous burden falls on the shoulders of the poor, and hence Sun Tzŭ concludes that to neglect the use of spies is nothing less than a crime against humanity.]

3. One who acts thus is no leader of men, no present help to his sovereign, no master of victory.

[This idea, that the true object of war is peace, has its root in the national temperament of the Chinese. Even so far back as 597 B.C., these memorable words were uttered by Prince Chuang of the Ch'u State: "The [Chinese] character for 'prowess' is made up of [the characters for] 'to stay' and 'a spear' (cessation of hostilities). Military prowess is seen in the repression of cruelty, the calling in of weapons, the preservation of the appointment of Heaven, the firm establishment of merit, the bestowal of happiness on the people, putting harmony between the princes, the diffusion of wealth."]

4. Thus, what enables the wise sovereign and the good general to strike and conquer, and achieve things beyond the reach of ordinary men, is *foreknowledge*.

[That is, knowledge of the enemy's dispositions, and what he means to do.]

5. Now this foreknowledge cannot be elicited from spirits; it cannot be obtained inductively from experience,

[Tu Mu's note is: "[knowledge of the enemy] cannot be gained by reasoning from other analogous cases."]

nor by any deductive calculation.

[Li Ch'uan says: "Quantities like length, breadth, distance and magnitude, are susceptible of exact mathematical determination; human actions cannot be so calculated."]

6. Knowledge of the enemy's dispositions can only be obtained from other men.

[Mei Yao-ch'en has rather an interesting note: "Knowledge of the spirit-world is to be obtained by divination; information in natural science may be sought by inductive reasoning; the laws of the universe can be verified by mathematical calculation: but the dispositions of an enemy are ascertainable through spies and spies alone."]

7. Hence the use of spies, of whom there are five classes: (1) Local spies; (2) inward spies; (3) converted spies; (4) doomed spies; (5) surviving spies.

8. When these five kinds of spy are all at work, none can discover the secret system. This is called "divine manipulation of the threads." It is the sovereign's most precious faculty.

["Cromwell, one of the greatest and most practical of all cavalry leaders, had officers styled 'scout masters,' whose business it was to collect all possible information regarding the enemy, through scouts and spies, etc., and much of his success in war was traceable to the previous knowledge of the enemy's moves thus gained."[1]]

9. Having *local spies* means employing the services of the inhabitants of a district.

[Tu Mu says: "In the enemy's country, win people over by kind treatment, and use them as spies."]

10. Having *inward spies*, making use of officials of the enemy.

[Tu Mu enumerates the following classes as likely to do good service in this respect: "Worthy men who have been degraded from office, criminals who have undergone punishment; also, favourite concubines who are greedy for gold, men who are aggrieved at being in subordinate positions, or who have been passed over in the distribution of posts, others who are anxious that their side should be defeated in order that they may have a

---

1. "Aids to Scouting," p. 2.

chance of displaying their ability and talents, fickle turncoats who always want to have a foot in each boat. Officials of these several kinds," he continues, "should be secretly approached and bound to one's interests by means of rich presents. In this way you will be able to find out the state of affairs in the enemy's country, ascertain the plans that are being formed against you, and moreover disturb the harmony and create a breach between the sovereign and his ministers." The necessity for extreme caution, however, in dealing with "inward spies," appears from an historical incident related by Ho Shih: "Lo Shang, Governor of I-Chou, sent his general Wei Po to attack the rebel Li Hsiung of Shu in his stronghold at P'i. After each side had experienced a number of victories and defeats, Li Hsiung had recourse to the services of a certain P'o-t'ai, a native of Wu-tu. He began to have him whipped until the blood came, and then sent him off to Lo Shang, whom he was to delude by offering to cooperate with him from inside the city, and to give a fire signal at the right moment for making a general assault. Lo Shang, confiding in these promises, march out all his best troops, and placed Wei Po and others at their head with orders to attack at P'o-t'ai's bidding. Meanwhile, Li Hsiung's general, Li Hsiang, had prepared an ambuscade on their line of march; and P'o-t'ai, having reared long scaling-ladders against the city walls, now lighted the beacon-fire. Wei Po's men raced up on seeing the signal and began climbing the ladders as fast as they could, while others were drawn up by ropes lowered from above. More than a hundred of Lo Shang's soldiers entered the city in this way, every one of whom was forthwith beheaded. Li Hsiung then charged with all his forces, both inside and outside the city, and routed the enemy completely." [This happened in 303 A.D. I do not know where Ho Shih got the story from. It is not given in the biography of Li Hsiung or that of his father Li T'e, *Chin Shu*, ch. 120, 121.]]

11. Having *converted spies*, getting hold of the enemy's spies and using them for our own purposes.

[By means of heavy bribes and liberal promises detaching them from the enemy's service, and inducing them to carry back false information as well as to spy in turn on their own countrymen. On the other hand, Hsiao Shih-hsien says that we pretend not to have detected him, but contrive to let him carry away a false impression of what is going on. Several of the commentators accept this as an alternative definition; but that it is not what Sun Tzŭ meant is conclusively proved by his subsequent remarks about treating the converted spy generously (§ 21 sqq.). Ho Shih notes three occasions on which converted spies were used with conspicuous success: (1) by T'ien Tan in his defence of Chi-mo (see *supra*, p. 90); (2) by Chao She on his march to O-yu (see p. 57); and by the wily Fan Chu in 260 B.C., when Lien P'o was conducting a defensive campaign against Ch'in. The King of Chao strongly disapproved of Lien P'o's cautious and dilatory methods, which had been unable to avert a series of minor disasters, and therefore lent a ready ear to the reports of his spies, who had secretly gone over to the enemy and were already in Fan Chu's pay. They said: "The only thing which causes Ch'in anxiety is lest Chao Kua should be made general. Lien P'o they consider an easy opponent, who is sure to be vanquished in the long run." Now this Chao Kua was a son of the famous Chao She. From his boyhood, he had been wholly engrossed in the study of war and military matters, until at last he came to believe that there was no commander in the whole Empire who could stand against him. His father was much disquieted by this overweening conceit, and the flippancy with which he spoke of such a serious thing as war, and solemnly declared that if ever Kua was appointed general, he would bring ruin on the armies of Chao. This was the man who, in spite of earnest protests from his own mother and the veteran statesman Lin Hsiang-ju, was now sent to succeed Lien P'o. Needless to say, he proved no match for the redoubtable Po Ch'i and the great military power of Ch'in. He fell into a trap by which his army was divided into two and his communications cut; and after a desperate resistance lasting 46 days, during which the famished soldiers devoured one another, he was himself killed by an arrow, and his whole force, amounting, it is said, to 400,000 men, ruthlessly put to the sword.]

12. Having *doomed spies*, doing certain things openly for purposes of deception, and allowing our own spies to know of them and report them to the enemy.

[Tu Yu gives the best exposition of the meaning: "We ostentatiously do things calculated to deceive our own spies, who must be led to believe that they have been unwittingly disclosed. Then, when these spies are captured in the enemy's lines, they will make an entirely false report, and the enemy will take measures accordingly, only to find that we do something quite different. The spies will thereupon be put to death." As an example of doomed spies, Ho Shih mentions the prisoners released by Pan Ch'ao in his campaign against Yarkand. (See p. 132.) He also refers to T'ang Chien, who in 630 A.D. was sent by T'ai Tsung to lull the Turkish Kahn Chieh-li into fancied security, until Li Ching was able to deliver a crushing blow against him. Chang Yu says that the Turks revenged themselves by killing T'ang Chien, but this is a mistake, for we read in both the old and the New T'ang History (ch. 58, fol. 2 and ch. 89, fol. 8 respectively) that he escaped and lived on until 656. Li I-chi played a somewhat similar part in 203 B.C., when sent by the King of Han to open peaceful negotiations with Ch'i. He has certainly more claim to be described a "doomed spy", for the king of Ch'i, being subsequently attacked without warning by Han Hsin, and infuriated by what he considered the treachery of Li I-chi, ordered the unfortunate envoy to be boiled alive.]

13. *Surviving spies*, finally, are those who bring back news from the enemy's camp.

[This is the ordinary class of spies, properly so called, forming a regular part of the army. Tu Mu says: "Your surviving spy must be a man of keen intellect, though in outward appearance a fool;

of shabby exterior, but with a will of iron. He must be active, robust, endowed with physical strength and courage; thoroughly accustomed to all sorts of dirty work, able to endure hunger and cold, and to put up with shame and ignominy." Ho Shih tells the following story of Ta'hsi Wu of the Sui dynasty: "When he was governor of Eastern Ch'in, Shen-wu of Ch'i made a hostile movement upon Sha-yuan. The Emperor T'ai Tsu [? Kao Tsu] sent Ta-hsi Wu to spy upon the enemy. He was accompanied by two other men. All three were on horseback and wore the enemy's uniform. When it was dark, they dismounted a few hundred feet away from the enemy's camp and stealthily crept up to listen, until they succeeded in catching the passwords used in the army. Then they got on their horses again and boldly passed through the camp under the guise of night-watchmen; and more than once, happening to come across a soldier who was committing some breach of discipline, they actually stopped to give the culprit a sound cudgeling! Thus they managed to return with the fullest possible information about the enemy's dispositions, and received warm commendation from the Emperor, who in consequence of their report was able to inflict a severe defeat on his adversary."]

14. Hence it is that with none in the whole army are more intimate relations to be maintained than with spies.

[Tu Mu and Mei Yao-ch'en point out that the spy is privileged to enter even the general's private sleeping-tent.]

None should be more liberally rewarded. In no other business should greater secrecy be preserved.

[Tu Mu gives a graphic touch: all communication with spies should be carried "mouth-to-ear." The following remarks on spies may be quoted from Turenne, who made perhaps larger use of them than any previous commander: "Spies are attached to those who give them most, he who pays them ill is never served. They should never be known to anybody; nor should they know one another. When they propose anything very material, secure their persons, or have in your possession their wives and children as hostages for their fidelity. Never communicate anything to them but what is absolutely necessary that they should know." [2]]

15. Spies cannot be usefully employed without a certain intuitive sagacity.

[Mei Yao-ch'en says: "In order to use them, one must know fact from falsehood, and be able to discriminate between honesty and double-dealing." Wang Hsi in a different interpretation thinks more along the lines of "intuitive perception" and "practical intelligence." Tu Mu strangely refers these attributes to the spies themselves: "Before using spies we must assure ourselves as to their integrity of character and the extent of their experience and skill." But he continues: "A brazen face and a crafty disposition are more dangerous than mountains or rivers; it takes a man of genius to penetrate such." So that we are left in some doubt as to his real opinion on the passage."]

16. They cannot be properly managed without benevolence and straightforwardness.

[Chang Yu says: "When you have attracted them by substantial offers, you must treat them with absolute sincerity; then they will work for you with all their might."]

17. Without subtle ingenuity of mind, one cannot make certain of the truth of their reports.

[Mei Yao-ch'en says: "Be on your guard against the possibility of spies going over to the service of the enemy."]

18. Be subtle! be subtle! and use your spies for every kind of business.

[Cf. VI. § 9.]

19. If a secret piece of news is divulged by a spy before the time is

---

2. "Marshal Turenne," p. 311.

ripe, he must be put to death together with the man to whom the secret was told.

[Word for word, the translation here is: "If spy matters are heard before [our plans] are carried out," etc. Sun Tzŭ's main point in this passage is: Whereas you kill the spy himself "as a punishment for letting out the secret," the object of killing the other man is only, as Ch'en Hao puts it, "to stop his mouth" and prevent news leaking any further. If it had already been repeated to others, this object would not be gained. Either way, Sun Tzŭ lays himself open to the charge of inhumanity, though Tu Mu tries to defend him by saying that the man deserves to be put to death, for the spy would certainly not have told the secret unless the other had been at pains to worm it out of him.]

20. Whether the object be to crush an army, to storm a city, or to assassinate an individual, it is always necessary to begin by finding out the names of the attendants, the aides-de-camp,

[Literally "visitors", is equivalent, as Tu Yu says, to "those whose duty it is to keep the general supplied with information," which naturally necessitates frequent interviews with him.]

the door-keepers and sentries of the general in command. Our spies must be commissioned to ascertain these.

[As the first step, no doubt towards finding out if any of these important functionaries can be won over by bribery.]

21. The enemy's spies who have come to spy on us must be sought out, tempted with bribes, led away and comfortably housed. Thus they will become converted spies and available for our service.

22. It is through the information brought by the converted spy that we are able to acquire and employ local and inward spies.

[Tu Yu says: "through conversion of the enemy's spies we learn the enemy's condition." And Chang Yu says: "We must tempt the converted spy into our service, because it is he that knows which of the local inhabitants are greedy of gain, and which of the officials are open to corruption."]

23. It is owing to his information, again, that we can cause the doomed spy to carry false tidings to the enemy.

[Chang Yu says, "because the converted spy knows how the enemy can best be deceived."]

24. Lastly, it is by his information that the surviving spy can be used on appointed occasions.

25. The end and aim of spying in all its five varieties is knowledge of the enemy; and this knowledge can only be derived, in the first instance, from the converted spy.

[As explained in §§ 22-24. He not only brings information himself, but makes it possible to use the other kinds of spy to advantage.]

Hence it is essential that the converted spy be treated with the utmost liberality.

26. Of old, the rise of the Yin dynasty

[Sun Tzŭ means the Shang dynasty, founded in 1766 B.C. Its name was changed to Yin by P'an Keng in 1401.]

was due to I Chih

[Better known as I Yin, the famous general and statesman who took part in Ch'eng T'ang's campaign against Chieh Kuei.]

who had served under the Hsia. Likewise, the rise of the Chou dynasty was due to Lü Ya

[Lu Shang rose to high office under the tyrant Chou Hsin, whom he afterwards helped to overthrow. Popularly known as T'ai Kung, a title bestowed on him by Wen Wang, he is said to have composed a treatise on war, erroneously identified with the *Liu T'ao*.]

who had served under the Yin.

[There is less precision in the Chinese than I have thought it well to introduce into my translation, and the commentaries on the passage are by no means explicit. But, having regard to the context, we can hardly doubt that Sun Tzŭ is holding up I Chih and Lu Ya as illustrious examples of the converted spy, or something closely analogous. His suggestion is, that the Hsia and Yin dynasties were upset owing to the intimate knowledge of their weaknesses and shortcoming which these former ministers were able to impart to the other side. Mei Yao-ch'en appears to resent any such aspersion on these historic names: "I Yin and Lu Ya," he says, "were not rebels against the Government. Hsia could not employ the former, hence Yin employed him. Yin could not employ the latter, hence Hou employed him. Their great achievements were all for the good of the people." Ho Shih is also indignant: "How should two divinely inspired men such as I and Lu have acted as common spies? Sun Tzŭ's mention of them simply means that the proper use of the five classes of spies is a matter which requires men of the highest mental caliber like I and Lu, whose wisdom and capacity qualified them for the task. The above words only emphasize this point." Ho Shih believes then that the two heroes are mentioned on account of their supposed skill in the use of spies. But this is very weak.]

27. Hence it is only the enlightened ruler and the wise general who will use the highest intelligence of the army for purposes of spying and thereby they achieve great results.

[Tu Mu closes with a note of warning: "Just as water, which carries a boat from bank to bank, may also be the means of sinking it, so reliance on spies, while production of great results, is oft-times the cause of utter destruction."]

Spies are a most important element in war, because on them depends an army's ability to move.

[Chia Lin says that an army without spies is like a man with ears or eyes.]